Praise for Crazy as Hell

"*Crazy as Hell* is just the antidote we need for these increasingly dumbed-down American times where books are (still) banned (stillborn) and crooked capitalist politicians continue to foment derision and division. Hoke S. Glover III and V. Efua Prince manage, in this blacker than Black book of so much light, to illuminate the subversive complexity of the soul of Black history, which is to say the soul of a nation that has been devoid of such conscientious Black contributions since its very founding. What makes this book sing and swing and marvel with magic is its built-in sense of humor and satire that is the heartbeat of the blues. Readers of all generations and backgrounds will enjoy these bite-sized fieldnotes by two artist-scholars on the frontline of what is necessary and what truly matters in setting the American record straight while telling it slant and meaningful as a gangsta lean. *Crazy as Hell* is woke before it was a verb or a noun and hijacked by bloviators making fascist statements dressed in bad ideas. It is a stroke of Black genius and critical race theory sans the pomposity and posturing and corny, dry-ass lingua franca of the academe machine."

—Tony Medina, author of *I Am Alfonso Jones* and
Thirteen Ways of Looking at a Black Boy

"More than just an extensive catalog of radiant, outlandish rule-breakers, this book offers a Black framework for thinking about, theorizing, celebrating, and critiquing cultural figures whose antics reside within the venerable crazy as hell tradition."

—Howard Rambsy II, author of *Bad Men:*
Creative Touchstones of Black Writers

"Um . . . this book, *Crazy as Hell*, is crazy as hell. Be careful while reading it. It might make you do something crazy as hell like demanding your human rights, developing a personal working definition of the concept of 'freedom,' daydreaming, or even thinking for yourself. Be careful." —Rion Amilcar Scott, author of *Insurrections* and
The World Doesn't Require You

Crazy as Hell

Crazy as Hell

W. W. NORTON & COMPANY

Independent Publishers Since 1923

Introduction by
Reginald Dwayne Betts

**The Best Little
Guide to Black History**

**Hoke S.
Glover III**

**V. Efua
Prince**

WE WANT TO ACKNOWLEDGE the many who read and commented on this work in progress, with particular thanks, in no particular order, to Valerie Jean, Virginia Spatz, Jacqueline Regina Blackwell, Reginald Dwayne Betts, the Wells Woodson group, Kwame Agyeman, Brian Gilmore, Natasha Tarpley, Marita Golden, Monifa Love, Candace Wiley, Nia Crawford, Jawanza Phoenix, Grace Deloris Stephenson, Marcus Graddy, Dennis Winston, David Green, Robert Watson, Richard and Perdita Spriggs, Asha French, Imani Bell, Elijah Prince, Garla Smith, Robert Sweeney, and Bob and Lurlene Sweeney. Very few were harmed in the making of this book, counting ourselves among the injured.

Public Service Announcement

THIS BOOK IS TERRIBLE. Our recommendation is that you do not read it, particularly if you are African American and already suffering with pre-existing conditions. Reading Black history can raise your blood pressure, which is bad for your health. What's worse is that, depending on how dark your humor, you will also find yourself laughing—ignorantly or inappropriately, depending on how you code switch. This is a particular hazard for Black people because, since the time of minstrel shows, laughing Black people have been looked upon with suspicion. So, if you insist on reading this book and you are Black, for the sake of the race, do not read it in church, in the library, at funerals, in prisons (Dwayne adding this because he believes it is not crazy as hell to center prison in his entire existence), or in other places where reverence is expected. It will have you laughing through tears.

FOR SAMUEL L. JACKSON
The quintessential on-screen badass who exemplifies
the *Crazy as Hell* spirit.

By the Last Remaining Heirs
of the Secret Love Child
of Mammy and Stagger Lee

Freedom is free of the need to be free.
Free your mind and your ass will follow.
The kingdom of heaven is within.
—Parliament Funkadelic

CONTENTS

Introduction by Reginald Dwayne Betts: Editor's Notes

A WOMAN I ONCE LOVED warned me that I can turn anything into heroin. She meant, more than that I had an addictive personality, that I was Crazy as Hell, and that crazy would make me cling on to whatever I imagined was the rickety raft that would save me.

Not for nothing, she ain't never lied. Crazy one of those things you can only understand through juxtaposition. When I was sixteen years old, I stood before a judge weighing in at 120 pounds and 5 feet 5 inches having gotten to sixteen after an impressive run of fisticuffs sparked by my sarcasm's inability to gauge the limitations of its wolf tickets.

I fucking love Black people is what I mean. The very contradiction of it. The first brother to punch me in the face in prison was a gang member; the second was a righteous Muslim. What we all shared was the proximity to handcuffs. And like the rest of the Black men in prison—except this stretch where I found myself on a prison in the gutted side of a mountain, run by white men who spoke a slang I'd never heard and on some days wielded shotguns and racism of the segregated South—mostly we feared what we might do to each other.

Surviving prison is Crazy as Hell. After being sentenced, I heard my Aunt Pandora, who once trusted me at twelve to watch her three children, scream like some wild and feral cat losing the last fight in an alley. "I'm aiight," I yelled back, sixteen and fragile and having read enough books to know how crazy it was to announce I'm a be aiight.

But I was, in a way. Inside learning what's in this book you hold. The stories that ain't make it into my grade school history courses became the secret knowledge that the brothers around me believed would make them righteous and scientific and powerful and freed by knowledge of self. And I wanted to be free like the rest of them, so I read it all, the books, the handwritten essays, the mimeographed texts.

And inside, I bartered and stole and hustled for more books. My canon was *The Destruction of Black Civilization* and *Wretched of the Earth* and *Every Shut Eye Ain't Asleep*. My heroes changed their names like Marvel characters: Leroi Jones witnessing his daughter peek into *her own clasped hands* becomes Amiri Baraka writing *I am inside someone / who hates me*. *Crazy as Hell* is about collapsing that distance, the alchemical way that Black folks have survived to answer the prayers of their children while feeling, like everybody does sometimes and maybe we do way more than sanity can stand, trapped inside someone (hmmm, America maybe) who hates us. One way to think of all of this is how crazy as hell it is to be Black in this country, even today, and figure out who you are.

One thing for certain, two things for sure, ain't nobody crazy enough to think a kid being hustled out of court in cuffs and shackles, headed to a prison cell, is safe.

As wild as it sounds though, I've always been safe between the pages of a book. Quiet as kept, the last book I checked out from the public library was *The Evelyn Wood Seven-Day Speed Reading and Learning Program*. Maybe I've always been convinced that if I lived between pages, even while in prison, for as long as I could, I'd find some safety.

Black in America means language is malleable. Niger becomes nigger becomes nigga becomes the paradox of juxtaposition. If you been African and Afro-American and African-American and Negro, you understand that flight is purely constrained by believing your wings don't work. That's why Toni Morrison said to fly you gotta let go of all the shit that's holding you down.

Crazy as Hell is an exploration. A map. When I met Hoke S. Glover III, co-creator of this book with Dr. V. Efua Prince, he was selling books off a cart outside of a gospel concert at Bowie State University.

And I was amped to be talking about books for the first time since prison. Hoke looked at me and asked, "So, where did you go to college?"

I was twenty-four years old and had been in the penitentiary since two weeks after my 11th-grade homecoming dance. I'd been home for less than thirty days and didn't even have a license. I tried to evade the question.

"I haven't graduated yet."

"Oh, so where *do* you go?"

"Look man, I just got out of prison."

What happened next is where I was introduced to crazy as hell. "So you're a poet," the brother with the long locs asked. And it's a wild question because I'd just told him, the first stranger I'd told, that I just came home from prison.

This book is an exploration of improvisation. Of how the central theme of Black survival here has been the invention of happenstance, which is to say crazy as hell—as a noun, adjective, and verb, suggests that liminal space where possibility becomes history.

Shit ain't always good either. When you're a people who were legally reduced to three-fifth, crazy as hell is where you begin if your start is the assertion that what happens next is homage to all the other crazy things we made actual to survive here.

This is a poet and a historian, a father, a mother, grandfather, a grandmother, educators, shit talkers, curators. But this book is also the barbershop and nail salon and that time I saw *Jitney* at Ford's Theatre filled with Black folks and at intermission two dozen brothers from ages twelve to eighty-seven talked about fatherhood and becoming and August Wilson and how crazy as hell it was that we were watching that show, free, on land where another white man imagined we'd be better off enslaved.

And we all showed up for Wilson, a Black man who tracked a century of life in this country without a single white character and proved it ain't crazy as hell to believe we matter enough to tell all of what got us here.

How to Read This Book

CRAZY AS HELL is a guide and not meant to be comprehensive. It captures the way Black people read each other and the crazy world we live in. Our ability to read well is key to surviving and thriving.

Just think about how much the phrase "crazy as hell" gets thrown around. We rarely mean that the person is clinically insane. We don't even mean the same thing every time we say it. You have to be able to hear the tone to understand the meaning. Moreover, the categories in *Crazy as Hell* are incomplete. We leave readers the freedom to figure out who is really crazy and who is not. Serial killers, for instance, are included here because they really are crazy, no doubt; but other categories of people, like rebellious people or people with anger issues, seem too close to home. That's the kind of crazy we recognize and are used to dealing with. We ask you to use a bit of introspection and self-analysis while reading. Think about the people you know. Think about yourself.

At times, *Crazy as Hell* invites you to look for more information, which is a fancy way of saying check out Wikipedia or Google. The problem is that algorithms reflect the biases of the people who made them. And for the most part, Black people ain't writing that code or written into that code. You can only find our shadows or rumors. Plus, typing a word or phrase into Google can come back with a hundred thousand results. You will need to think the way slaves thought when deciding to trust some information. Major news outlets often fail but usually make an effort to be fair and balanced. They hire diversity people to help them with that. Schools often have enormous blind spots, but they try to be representative by vetting information through a process known as "peer review," which helps them present balanced information. Companies have to make profits to please shareholders, but good information can come from well-funded and well-meaning corporations. Follow the advice my grandmother gave: Consider the source.

Foreword

MAKING A LITTLE BOOK ON BLACK HISTORY is difficult. In many respects, African Americans are even more a symbol of the country's continuing oppression than Native Americans. Though our time here has been short compared to theirs, our influence on the world stage often seems more significant. African Americans influence the world because America influences the world.

Crazy as Hell is a short and simple [EDITOR'S NOTE: NAH NOT SIMPLE, AIN'T NOTHING ABOUT BEING BLACK IN AMERICA EVER BEEN SIMPLE] Black fact book that challenges the traditional view of African American history as a somber and often depressing category, full of tales of oppression. Discrimination, racism, lynchings, and police brutality are all important parts of our history, but they are not definitive. You ever heard of Michael Jordan flying—and not just to the hoop? Or that brother named Charles Drew who did whatever it took to make blood transfusions possible, only to die because white folks wouldn't use his invention on him? Black people encounter oppression but are not solely defined by it. Our *Crazy as Hell* notables are tragic in their humanity and transcend the boundaries defined by being Black in America.

All of humanity is tragic, bloodied, and beautiful. Black history heroes often make it to history books for symbolizing the opposite of what people think we are. The problem, of course, is that it is all too easy to imagine Black people as less than we are. In this way our heroes become imbalanced and often achieve a perfection that seems real only when it is juxtaposed to a false image.

The luminaries here are, without a doubt, remarkable, but they are also crazy as hell. This collection of short stories and facts reveals that Black history heroes are everyday people who, in their humanity, made history simply by being themselves.

As for their actual insanity, we leave that judgment to the reader. But insanity and blackness have been wedded in America since slavery. A slave who sought freedom was working against white supremacy's designated natural order that stated that the conquered were conquered because they were less than the conquerors. In that way, this book is spiritual. To find truth of freedom, defy the odds, and work toward liberation, one must first have the thought before it will come into being. In that way, every enslaved person who dreamt of freedom dreamt an original Crazy as Hell thought.

If Black people were not so crazy, we would not even share this book with you. But given the circumstances, we feel compelled to offer it to you. Maybe once you read it, you will notice the crazy in your community and in the world and understand that just because *you* are crazy doesn't mean you can't be a part of Black history too. You can. This whole country is Crazy as Hell.

The Runaway

RUNAWAYS ARE TRICKY. We all want to run away from something. Some of us follow through with it. Some of us don't. But all of us have dreamed of turning tail and cutting out. For enslaved African Americans, running was a natural response to the problem of slavery. (Why you think we so good at track and field?) Regardless of how common the impulse was to run, most people didn't. Living in the twenty-first century might make it difficult for us to understand just how Crazy enslaved folks had to be to run away. But for one reason or another, these runaways can't stay. And for us, their running harnesses the power of flight.

PUBLIC SERVICE ANNOUNCEMENT
Running away is a type of change. Change is hard for most people to accept. Most won't run away. They'll work that job they hate forever and drink more Crown Royal and cheat on their partner before they think about running to get to freedom.

Harriet Tubman

GIVEN WHAT WE KNOW ABOUT SLAVERY, anyone who ever escaped from the grip of the slaveholding South had to be Crazy as Hell to ever risk going back! But not only did Harriet Tubman go back south, she did it at least nineteen times! Sometimes she even used insanity as a disguise. She'd dress in a raggedy hooded garment to appear like a mentally impaired man. She spoke in tongues and acted like an old woman chasing a chicken. And everybody knows that when you see an old woman chasing a chicken you just gotta let her keep doing what she's doing.

Her famous efforts in leading over eight hundred fugitives to freedom earned her the moniker "Moses," after the Old Testament hero. In 1868, another of our Crazy as Hell heroes, Frederick Douglass, wrote to Tubman of her exploits as a conductor for the Underground Railroad: "You . . . have labored in a private way. I have wrought in the day—you the night . . . while the most that you have done has been witnessed by a few trembling, scared, and foot-sore bondmen and women whom you have led out of the house of bondage, and whose heartfelt 'God bless you' has been your only reward."

We got her listed here, but she really is an OG. Tubman served as a nurse and a spy during the Civil War, and she was the first African American woman to direct a military campaign. In 1896, on land near her home in Auburn, New York, Tubman established the Harriet Tubman Home for the Aged. When she died, in 1913, she was buried with military honors. But what's really crazy as hell is that Tubman's Home for the Aged is two miles from New York's first prison, meaning she might still be bringing African American folks to freedom. She's the stuff of legends. Look her up.

Frederick Douglass

FREDERICK DOUGLASS WAS the most well-known anybody of his day. What did he do? He was a fugitive slave who taught himself to read and write; he wrote three classics, starting with *Narrative of the Life of Frederick Douglass*; became one of the most sought after abolitionists; was literally the most photographed person of his era; and, if that wasn't enough, after his Black wife died, he married a white woman! You know how folks act when a Black man marries a white woman now; imagine how they acted in the nineteenth century. He *had* to be crazy. But the craziest thing Frederick Douglass did was fighting his enslaver Mr. Covey, which some might say wasn't really all that crazy since Covey kept beating on Douglass to begin with. After that, running away seems like a natural next step. That is the way it usually happened for Black people in the South—you got fed up with mistreatment, beat the master's ass, then hauled tail before the Massa gathered his posse and started stringing folks up.

The way Douglass tells it, in 1833 a white man who believed he was Douglass's master told him he was being sent to work for Edward Covey, a poor farmer, for a year—unpaid, of course. Covey worked hard, sometimes alongside his hired (or enslaved) hands, but he was brutal and vicious. He beat Douglass weekly for six months until Douglass collapsed from exhaustion. Unmoved, Covey tried to force Douglass to work through his weariness. Douglass instead hid in the cornfields until he came across a freeman named Sandy Jenkins. Jenkins gave him a conjure root to keep on his right side that would prevent any white man from assaulting him again. (If y'all don't know about roots, you should look them up.) The root proved true, or at least Douglass's hands did, because less than a day later, when Covey came with a rope to tie Douglass to the whipping post, Douglass resisted. For two hours the men fought before Covey relented. Let's just say this: He never whipped Douglass again.

Margaret Garner

P. S. BASSETT OF THE FAIRMOUNT THEOLOGICAL SEMINARY interviewed Margaret Garner on February 12, 1856, in the cell where she was being held. Garner nursed her infant baby while she described how she had hit two of her children on the head with shovels and slashed another's throat after slave hunters found her as a fugitive. Can you imagine the kind of gift her kids gave her for Mother's Day? Oh, wait. She was enslaved. Toni Morrison fictionalized Garner's story in the acclaimed novel *Beloved*. Garner is an important historical figure because she was enslaved on a small farm near Cincinnati, where slavery was supposed to be mild. Ain't that crazy as hell? The very notion of a *mild* form of slavery? But that's what they say about Ohio because it wasn't the Deep South. Yet clearly she'd rather kill her children than allow them to be returned to slavery. Infanticide seems crazy, but even Garner's mother-in-law (the children's grandmother who had eight children of her own snatched from her by slavery) refused to condemn the act. For what it's worth though, it seems kinda important to note that if this logic prevailed, African Americans would have been wiped out by the hand of their own mothers.

Henry "Box" Brown

HOW ABOUT UPS-ING or Fedex-ing yourself from prison? You might think that is crazy as hell, but that's what Henry "Box" Brown did. On March 23, 1849, Henry was shipped from Richmond, Virginia, to Philadelphia in a box labeled "dry goods." He got help from two friends who happened to have the same last name: a Black man named James Caeser Anthony Smith and a white sympathizer who liked to gamble named Samuel Alexander Smith. They thought the whole matter worked so well that they did it again. Later both men were arrested after trying to mail slaves. But get this: only the white man served time. James Smith got off and joined Brown in Boston. Brown later made a living doing a traveling stage show where he told his story and reenacted parts of his journey to freedom. Stories of runaways are always crazy, but this is one of the craziest. Note: The trip took twenty-seven hours. There's no bathroom in a UPS box. Figure it out. Yeah. Crazy as hell.

Gladys Bentley

ALTHOUGH GEORGE SAND MAY HAVE DISAGREED, some say that the term "cross-dressing" was invented to describe Gladys Bentley. Bentley ran away from home and found herself earning a living as a lesbian performer in the clubs of Harlem. She'd dress in a white tuxedo and top hat. In the early twentieth century, a person who broke with conventional norms of dress tended to be seen as crazy. Nevertheless, her performances attracted the attention of Harlem's artists and intellectuals, like Langston Hughes. As society became increasingly repressive during the latter decades of her life—the late 1940s and 1950s—Bentley was compelled to deny her sexual orientation to get work. But before that, she earned a reputation for playing popular songs while improvising risqué lyrics.

Deadbeat Dads

THOUGH THIS IS NOT one particular person, the term is so popular, we had to include it. During slavery times, Black men got studded out to make more babies so that the Massa in charge could make more money. Afterward, that same man might be sold to another plantation. Slavery tried to eradicate the bonds of family, love, marriage, and paternity. What's more, after tearing Black men away from their families, the Massa could imagine himself as a father to everybody on the plantation—which is crazy as hell. Then too, the master was the biological father of many Black people. There are many stories of masters who actually served as father to their mulatto children, but then other masters were like the ultimate deadbeat dads, imagining their children as less than human. Black fathers who run away are a category: my-baby's-father, my-baby-daddy, the-dude-that-don't-pay-child-support, the I-don't-know-where-he's-at, I-ain't-spoken-to-him, I-never-met-him, I-don't-even-know-who-he-is. It might sound crazy, but one way to look at Deadbeat Dads is like the runaways who kept running away even after slavery was over.

More on the Runaway

- Read *Narrative of the Life of Frederick Douglass, an American Slave* or check out the speech Douglass gave on July 5, 1852, called "What to the Slave is the Fourth of July?"

- Harriet Jacobs' *Incidents in the Life of a Slave Girl* was, like Douglass's autobiography, written in the nineteenth century but from a woman's perspective.

- Toni Morrison's *Beloved* is called a neo-slave narrative because it imagines what slavery must have been like for women like Margaret Garner.

- Visit the Harriet Tubman Underground Railroad Byway on Maryland's Eastern Shore.

- Project Gutenberg digitized a lot of old books and made them available for free online, among them *Narrative of Henry Box Brown*.

The Rebel

IT IS COMMON TO HEAR folks talk about fighting and resisting, which is why that Public Enemy song "Fight the Power" became an instant classic. But talking about rebelling is different than taking up arms in defense of human rights. Today, Black people think you crazy if you do anything that might increase the risk for premature death—particularly if you end up dying while fighting against the odds. One of the primary lessons of slavery is surviving to live another day. Rebels didn't learn that lesson. They might even *choose* to die. Most of us would say that's crazy as hell.

PUBLIC SERVICE ANNOUNCEMENT
If you weren't leading no rebellions before you picked up this book, don't try to lead one now. The difficulty with rebellions is that sometimes, maybe a lot of times, folks can't figure out what side they're on, or they can't stop rebelling once they start. Rebellions should overturn oppressive conditions. But we don't always distinguish between everyday difficulties encountered walking through life and systemic obstacles designed by authorities to keep us from progressing. Authority can be a good thing when it operates in the best interest of the community.

Nat Turner

NAT TURNER HEARD VOICES! How many of *you* hear voices? Another of our *Crazy as Hell* heroes, Malcolm X, had a vision of Nation of Islam leader Elijah Muhammad while he was in prison, and *Crazy as Hell* shero Sojourner Truth claimed to have heard from God's spirit, but that ain't really the same as hearing voices. When he was a young man, Turner ran away from his plantation in Southampton, Virginia, but returned because he had a vision from God calling him to do great and important work. That mission was to slay his enemies with their own weapons. So Turner mobilized over seventy enslaved people and freedmen to launch an assault on August 21, 1831. A solar eclipse earlier in the year was the sign that the time was soon coming. In the end, Nat Turner and his band killed sixty white men, women, and children. Like slaveholders, they did not discriminate based on gender or age. Most of us would call anyone crazy who said that the answer to their prayers was a message from God telling them to kill their masters.

Denmark Vesey

NOT MUCH IS KNOWN ABOUT DENMARK VESEY. We do know that he was a literate slave, like another of our *Crazy as Hell* heroes, Nat Turner. And we know that more than a hundred years later, a white supremacist would slaughter nine people at Vesey's church, Mother Emanuel AME in Charleston, SC. You can look it up if you want to know more about the connection.

Denmark Vesey won the Powerball in the South Carolina State Lottery in 1800, purchased his freedom, and began stockpiling weapons and organizing folks for a slave revolt. Of course, we're kidding. There wasn't a Powerball back then. But the rest is true. At the age of thirty-two, Vesey purchased his freedom with $600 after winning $1,500 in a lottery. Think about that. Black folks play their numbers *today*—trying to win the lottery so they can purchase their economic freedom.

Vesey's real claim to fame, and what makes him crazy as hell, was his organizing what many consider to be the largest plan for a slave revolt in the history of the country. It is said that as he planned the revolt, Vesey even sent word to Haiti to begin to set up international relations.

Father Moses Dickson

BORN FREE IN CINCINNATI, OHIO, on April 4, 1824, Moses Dickson organized the Knights of Liberty, twelve men who grew in ten years into an army of 42,000 men. They prepared a national insurrection against southern slaveholders in July 1857. They were armed and ready to go, but on the eve of the attack, Dickson called it off. He sensed growing tensions between the North and South. He told the Knights of Liberty to be patient and to trust God. He even went to talk to John Brown to try to get him to call off the raid at Harpers Ferry. Is it crazy to think about a Black freeman risking his life for enslaved people, most of whom he would never meet? He was committed to the cause. He did a lot of other things, too. Throughout the 1850s, Dickson was a conductor for the Underground Railroad. He made escape plans, harbored fugitives, and raised money. He told a reporter for the *Denver Post* that some of the biggest donors were slave owners who did not believe in slavery. *Enslavers. Who. Did. Not. Believe. In. Slavery.* Can you believe that?

Gabriel Prosser

MAYBE BECAUSE HE COULDN'T MANAGE the contradictions of being born into slavery in 1776 in Henrico County, Virginia, this man was crazy enough to organize his own revolution. We know this brotha was crazy because after Gabriel, his brother Solomon, and another slave were caught stealing a pig, Gabriel wrestled the white overseer to the ground and bit off his ear! We get being hungry enough to steal a pig—but he was hungry enough to eat a white man's ear. (Mighta been ancestor to crazy as hell Mike Tyson.) After that, they would have executed Gabriel, but there was an exception in the law that said that if the convicted could recite a verse from the Bible, he would receive a public branding. Reciting Bible verses was easy for Gabriel, so instead of killing him, they branded his hand. In hindsight, I'm sure they wished they had gone on and executed him. Cause for Gabriel, the public branding thing was the last straw. Gabriel started planning open rebellion. And if it hadn't stormed so badly the day it was set to take place, he might have had more success. Google Gabriel Prosser to get more details on who betrayed him.

Robert Williams

IN 1955 ROBERT WILLIAMS rose to the presidency of a flailing NAACP branch in Monroe, North Carolina. It had just six members when he was voted to lead it. The organization was dying because white aggression against the NAACP increased across the South following the 1954 *Brown vs. Board of Education, Topeka, Kansas* Supreme Court decision. This increased scrutiny scared off nearly all the bougie Black folks who used to fill the roster of the Monroe branch. But Williams was a WWII veteran who was like a pit bull defending his home ever since Uncle Sam commissioned him to kill for democratic principles overseas. Fighting a war can make you a little crazy. But Williams was so crazy that he stood outside a funeral parlor alongside three dozen other men with rifles, all aiming their carbines at a motorcade of marauding Klansmen to protect the body of a man who had already been executed for murder. Yeah. The man was *already dead*. Check out the documentary *Negroes with Guns: Rob Williams and Black Power* to learn more about him.

More on the Rebel

- Check out history.com, nationalgeographic.com, nationalhumanitiescenter.org, and the Library of Congress's African American Odyssey.

- Visit the Smithsonian Institute's National Museum of American History and National Museum of African American History and Culture.

- Watch the documentary *Negroes with Guns: Rob Williams and Black Power.*

- David Robertson wrote a book called *Denmark Vesey: The Buried Story of America's Largest Slave Revolt and the Man Who Led it.*

- The Voice of Cincinnati has a website with information on Father Moses Dickson if you want to check out more information on him.

- And the PBS Resource Bank has a teacher's guide with information on Gabriel Prosser.

The Mythic Negro

WHEN WE GOT HERE, African mythology was within us, but a slave ship is obscenely different than anything experienced in Africa. The journey across the Middle Passage was crazy as hell. It was near impossible for Africans coming from dozens of cultures and languages to retain whatever mythologies had sustained them before the boat, making it hard for the mythology of any of Africa's many ethnic groups to become the one African American mythology.

Before Wakanda and Black Panther, everyday Black folks told old tales about Black superheroes: normal, everyday Black folks who somehow beat slavery and Massa. Black mythic heroes show the natural ability to outwit oppression.

African American mythology is not simply about remembering history. The stories show how the ability to be crazy, act crazy, or ignore crazy has helped us survive. The mythical heroes who seem crazy help us deal with the times we feel sad, lonely, and like we are going crazy. The stories of rebels, outlaws, and runaways have become mythic. We admire them in their resistance and for their audacity to do what many of us are scared to do.

PUBLIC SERVICE ANNOUNCEMENT

The supernatural and myths can be dangerous. Hoteps, Wakandans, and Black folks who believe in something else often change myths to suit their purposes. We think they crazy as hell. Maybe they are. Maybe they aren't. But remember this: if you change your myths, you change what you believe.

Black Folks Who Jumped Off the Boat

SHOULD YOU STAY ON THE BOAT or jump overboard? This is where things start. People always joke that they "wouldn't have been no slave," and Kanye West (who's crazy as hell) took a lot of flak for saying slavery was a choice. Let's pretend for a moment that Kanye ain't cray cray and think about it for a moment. Is it crazier to be a slave or jump off the boat and die? Only you can answer that question for yourself.

You shouldn't read a piece of Black literature about slavery without remembering Black people who jumped off a slave ship. Slave ships were hell with sails—full of sickness, filth, rape, and shackles. Slave ships crossing the Atlantic had mortality rates averaging between 10 and 20 percent. That means a lot of the folks who got on the boat didn't make it here. Sure, it's crazy as hell to jump off a boat in the middle of the ocean, but the fact that many of the people in the Maafa did it makes you think about how bad slavery was. Then again, maybe it's crazy as hell to stay on the boat thinking, "Sure, it's bad now, but after we get off this boat, it'll be alright."

Br'er Rabbit

THE FIGURE OF BR'ER (BROTHER) RABBIT is an African retention, which is something that endured the Middle Passage and remained part of the culture. He is a trickster figure who outsmarts people who are bigger and stronger than him. He knows how to be slick enough to get what he wants. Br'er Rabbit is like the original Black myth getting his hustle on. He's smart and under the radar. His opponents are often animal versions of Massa: predators, like a fox or a bear. Sometimes the animals get together to catch Br'er Rabbit. But Br'er Rabbit always manages to escape from whatever mess he finds himself in. While Br'er Rabbit descends directly from West Africa, the best-known depiction in American culture is Bugs Bunny. Yeah, the "What's up, doc?" rabbit. Bugs Bunny is a trickster, running around always outsmarting Elmer Fudd and whatnot. He ain't no European invention. He was taken, the same way white musicians put their spin on Black music. You probably didn't know that because cultural appropriation doesn't acknowledge the source, which is why taking someone else's culture is so problematic. There is probably not a single Black person who ever got paid a dime off of Br'er Rabbit stories, while, beginning with Joel Chandler Harris, entire industries have built fortunes off of them—which is crazy as hell. White people used the trickster as a trick to make more money. Now ain't *that* a stinker!

High John the Conqueror

IT MAY SOUND CRAZY, but High John the Conqueror is the real time slavery superhero. Before there was television, Luke Cage, and Marvel, Black folks would tell stories about this former African prince who was sold into slavery, married the devil's daughter, and always outwitted Massa. And that's just his Tuesday! Zora Neale Hurston said High John the Conqueror's most powerful weapon was laughter. Laughter and a smile seem crazy when someone's mad at you or trying to take something from you or trying to beat you, but that kind of crazy is part of what protected us. Honestly, you can put this tactic into practice at any time. It's very simple: Start by making sure you are wearing your best running shoes, in case things go awry. Then, after reading these next few sentences, put the book down and find people to piss off. When they are thoroughly enraged, take a deep breath and laugh at them as loud or as heartily as you can. You'll be surprised at the relieving effects a little laughter can have on your personal psyche, and there's a chance the person you are dealing with will realize a very important lesson as well! Cuz laughter says there's something deeper than what you got to deal with. Things might seem crazy as hell, but like High John the Conqueror, you can know trouble don't last always. Google "High John the Conqueror"; there's gonna be some oils and roots that come up, but keep going until you get to the stories. Go read one.

Anansi the Spider (Aunt Nancy)

ANANSI IS THE ASHANTI AFRICAN GOD OF STORYTELLING who outwits more powerful beings, usually for selfish gain. In West Africa, Anansi is a trickster who acts as go-between for Nyame the sky god and humans. In fact, it was Anansi who approached Nyame to give people rain and night. After crossing the Atlantic with Africans during the Middle Passage, Anansi got off the boat in the Gullah regions of Georgia and South Carolina as Aunt Nancy, a spider woman whose wit and smarts gained her the upper hand. Even though she could seem like just another poor old Black woman in the South, her clever words—and sometimes crooked deeds—were effective, which is why she still around. If you look carefully, you can find Aunt Nancy stories in books, television, and folktales. We all have an Aunt Nancy in our lives. Look hard enough and she'll be there getting over on the system. Bonus points if you can't find an example of her in your life because that means *you* probably the Aunt Nancy!

John Henry

MOST AFRICAN AMERICANS KNOW the story of John Henry. Folks told the story to their children, sang John Henry work songs, and when we were no longer performing hard labor, we made John Henry picture books for schoolchildren to check out of the library. As the story goes, John Henry was born with a hammer in his hand, he was bigger than most children, and as he came of age, he could work harder than anybody. In the end, John Henry raced a machine that did the same work that he did. He beat the machine, and then he died. It's crazy, but this is the earliest recorded Black-guy-always-dies-before-the-end-of-the-story trope. Scott Reynolds Nelson tracked down records of a guy named John Williams Henry. He published a book in 2006 called *Steel Drivin' Man: John Henry: The Untold Story of an American Legend* where he claims John Henry was actually a prisoner in Virginia who had been leased out by the warden to help build the Lewis Tunnel in Millsboro, Virginia. The thing is, everybody knows a John Henry. Africans were brought here to work hard, and in some cases, plantations worked Black folks literally to death. It's sorta crazy that we got a story about somebody beating the machine and dying—and then still believe in hard work like we do. Some folks got three jobs. Part-time jobs, little jobs on the side, hustles. Most Black folks believe in staying on the grind and putting in work. But if there's a lesson to learn from John Henry, always remember you crazy as hell if you think you can beat the machine. You might beat the machine, but you'll die winning.

Hustlers and Drug Dealers

THERE'S A FAMOUS OLD BOOK you should check out by Sam Greenlee called *The Spook Who Sat by the Door*. Greenlee wrote it in 1968, during the Black Power times when Black folks believed in revolution. In the book, Dan Freeman hustles his way to a job with the CIA and then uses the knowledge he gains to wage war on them. Problem is, everybody's cousin think they somebody's spook by the door. Black folks working for white people almost always think some secret activity we doing at the office is going to change the world. But when Friday comes, it's a missing check (not the world not changing) that makes a brother lose the rest of his mind.

Hustlers, drug dealers, and super criminals are the opposite of the spook by the door. Perhaps Pablo Escobar is the best example. He ain't even Black, but he's been named-dropped by more rappers than a Baptist preacher says Jesus on a Sunday morning, so yes, we'll invite him to the cookout. *Say hello to my little friend. Scarface*'s Tony Montana is another example of the crazy-as-hell-drug-dealing-mobster some Black folks admire. He ain't even Black, which should make us pause for a minute. Maybe we aren't the original criminals, hustlers, and drug dealers. Yeah. Crazy as hell. And we all know drug dealers are bad for the Black community. It's crazy as hell how we make folks who sell drugs to Black people into heroes. Biggie Smalls got a song called the "Ten Crack Commandments"—but the dealers be the ones throwing money around and supporting folks. They drop so much cash in neglected communities that folks buy into the myth that doing good acts can clean blood money.

Revolutionaries

REVOLUTIONARIES ARE ALWAYS crazy as hell. There are many of them throughout this book. Many of them wrote books, staged protests, and fought the power. Some of them actually killed white folks. Others wrote books about how Black folks could get free.

But here's the thing: Most Black folks don't wanna be a revolutionary because the stuff revolutionaries be saying is pretty crazy. Black freedom and Black thought have always been close to crazy. Think about it: As far back as the early nineteenth century, David Walker had to sew the pamphlets he wrote into the lining of clothing to keep white people from reading them before he could get them to folks enslaved in the South. And he still died under mysterious circumstances.

Our life expectancy is already pretty low. Many of us still so scared that we whisper every time we say the words "white people." One could even say revolutionaries are technically unemployed since they have never actually been successful at their jobs. After all, Black people still talk about trying to get to freedom. Most Black folks think making a living and surviving is much more important than teaching others how to think right and set the history books straight. We might listen to a revolutionary every once in a while, but we usually blow them off. We be like, "Yeah, whatever, you know they crazy as hell. I gotta go to work."

Mammy

THE MYTHIC FIGURE OF MAMMY is a product of the antebellum South. Mammy is a Black woman who cook and clean better than anybody. She is dark-skinned, heavy-set, has her head wrapped in a handkerchief knotted in the front, and wears a dress and apron. Mammy is important because white people love her. She serve white folks well. And she love white folks way more than she love herself, which is crazy as hell. Her presence in white households frees the mistress from the messier aspects of home life and raising children, without the threat of her ever becoming the master's side chick. The stereotypical Mammy does not have, nor does she want, intimate relationships or biological children. She doesn't want money or vacations. While she may be headstrong, Mammy is tolerable because she has no ambitions apart from nurturing the white family she serves. In creating the myth of Mammy, white folks tried to make serving them into an art. Maybe in the end the slave, nigger, and Mammy are the greatest pieces of art white folks ever created.

Jack Beat the Devil

JACK IS CRAZY AS HELL, first and foremost because he played cards with the Devil. Secondly because he thought he could win. He doesn't win, of course, because, well, who can beat the Devil? When Jack's gamble doesn't pay off, he gets real sad, like a Black man who lost his job. He is man enough to take the Devil on and baby enough to cry when his luck runs out. But Jack survives by finding favor with wiser, older men or with the Devil's daughter, who offer him instructions— usually some crazy ritual like feeding a young bull to an eagle to catch a ride on its back across an ocean, or walking backward nine steps, then throwing sand over his shoulders. These rituals work to change Jack's fortunes, or at the very least they buy him time—which is all Jack really needs. Jack doesn't plan too far ahead. Instead, he lives from moment to moment. Jack is the workaday Black man who don't got no job, is a bit unreliable, and can't help anyone but himself. He finds ways to enjoy himself despite the fact that he has been handed the least enjoyable place in society. Perhaps he takes risks because he has so little to lose. Ultimately, Jack takes the Devil on so many twists and turns that the Devil winds up breaking his own neck. Jack beats the Devil by managing to survive.

More on the Mythic Negro

- A good place to begin is with Zora Neale Hurston's collection of oral histories and folk songs passed down from enslaved people called *Mules and Men.*

- Virginia Hamilton wrote a favorite children's story called *The People Who Could Fly: American Black Folktales,* illustrated by Leo and Diane Dillon.

- *From My People: 400 Years of African American Folklore, An Anthology* is, like Hurston's book, a collection of African American folk wisdom, edited by Daryl Cumber Dance.

- For more stories, try *Talk That Talk: An Anthology of African-American Storytelling,* edited by Linda Gross.

- *Dark Matter: A Century of Speculative Fiction from the African Diaspora,* edited by Sheree Renée Thomas, showcases modern Black writers at their most creative.

- Check out the art by Betye Saar and Kara Walker.

The Inmate

MOST AFRICAN AMERICANS DESCEND from people who were kidnapped from Africa and brought in chains across the Atlantic Ocean. In Africa they were fully human, but in the United States of America, they were considered something less. They were traded as property and forced to work as slaves. Certainly, people who were forced to work under these conditions must have thought a lot of wild things. Like when that white man cracked a whip and called him "nigger," the Black man thought, "I got your *nigger* right here," or "That ain't what your mama said to me last night." But the craziest thing a slave could think is "I wanna be free." Slaves ain't free!

That kind of slavery ended with President Abraham Lincoln. During the Civil War in 1863, Lincoln wrote the Emancipation Proclamation. Then at the end of the Civil War, he signed the 13th Amendment into law, and 3.9 million slaves were free. Since that time, the only way to force people into involuntary servitude is by locking them up. Now, instead of slavery, America boasts the world's largest prison industrial complex, with 25 percent of the world's prison population. Today, Black people make up 13 percent of the US population but 37 percent of people in prison. Clearly, there's a connection between slavery and the modern penal system, but you gotta admit that some of the folks in prison are crazy as hell.

PUBLIC SERVICE ANNOUNCEMENT
Black people are divided about questions of freedom when it comes to prison. Some consider it the worst thing in the world. Others think it is inevitable that many of us are gonna get locked up. Part of the reason folks are so twisted about incarceration has to do with how crazy some of the reasons are for folks being locked up. Look up the "Black Codes" that were put in place after Emancipation to see how all of this mess got started.

Etheridge Knight

POET ETHERIDGE KNIGHT IS ONE OF THE BEST EXAMPLES of locked-up genius. He was born in Corinth, Mississippi, on April 19, 1931. Knight dropped out of high school, joined the Army, and fought in the Korean War. On the back of his first book he claimed, "I died in Korea from a shrapnel wound, and narcotics resurrected me. I died in 1960 from a prison sentence and poetry brought me back to life." Google his poem "Feeling Fucked Up." Read it and you might imagine he was hip-hop before hip-hop was born. Many of us, especially if we listen to hip-hop, know what it is like to feel fucked up or do some fucked-up shit; but like Etheridge, we move in and out of that feeling. We don't stay there. We do some things that ain't good, and we do other things that are beautiful.

In another famous poem called "Hardrock Returns from the Hospital for the Criminal Insane," he tells the story of a Black hero prisoner who wouldn't take no trash. In the poem, Hardrock is returning from the mental ward with his mind broken. Before he went, he was one of the strongest and most resistant men around. At the hospital, they literally cut out part of his brain to make him less of a man. Imagine an African American poet writing a poem about that and winning awards for it. That's crazy as hell. Knight did eight years in prison for robbery. Afterward, he went on to win a list of prestigious awards for poetry, including a Guggenheim Fellowship. He also struggled with addiction and received a degree in criminal justice in 1990. Yeah, the former criminal gets a degree in criminal justice. Crazy as hell.

Detroit Red aka Satan aka Malcolm X aka El Hajj Malik El Shabazz

MALCOLM X WOULD SAY THINGS in public everybody else was scared to say. For this reason, we consider him as fearless and also crazy as hell. In Black history, the two categories almost always go together. Black people, for the most part, think you crazy as hell if you change your name or if you join the Nation of Islam. This brotha changed his name like four times *and* joined the Nation of Islam! The Nation of Islam is a Black nationalist organization that invented the tactic of naming the white man the Devil. It's sorta brilliant if you think about it, but it's crazy as hell to run around calling white folks the Devil if you expect to get a job. Obviously, Malcolm wasn't looking for a job.

Think about the names he called himself. When he was on the streets doing robberies and using drugs, Malcolm took the name "Detroit Red." In *The Autobiography of Malcolm X*, he said he was so mean when he got to prison that they called him Satan. Yeah, Satan. The Devil. And if that don't sound crazy enough, the Honorable Elijah Muhammad, founder of the Nation of Islam, came to him in a dream before he ever met him. (Yeah, you decide whether you want to believe it or not.) Couple years later, the dude was making Black history: he was famous, on TV, and running around calling the white man the Devil. Crazy as hell. You can find a ton of stuff online about Malcolm X.

Mumia Abu-Jamal

IT IS HARD IN BLACK HISTORY to figure out where crazy begins and ends. Obviously, any country that talks about freedom while they have you enslaved is crazy as hell. Get this. Journalist Mumia Abu-Jamal isn't really crazy, but his story, like that of other Black political prisoners, is. He was born April 24, 1954. Jamal was convicted and sentenced to death in 1982 for the murder of police officer David Faulkner. In 2001, his death sentence was overturned but he is still in prison now under a sentence of life without parole. While in prison, Mumia continued to work as a journalist. Years ago, you could ride to work and listen to his radio program that begins, "This is Mumia Abu-Jamal live from death row." Live from death row, reporting from prison. He's still reporting today. This man really took "don't quit your day job" to a whole new level. That's crazy as hell.

George Jackson

WHEN YOU GOOGLE A PICTURE of George Jackson, you see a man in shackles with a beautiful Afro and a fit frame. Although he spent most of his adult life in prison, in the days of Black Power in the late sixties, Jackson was one of the most iconic Black revolutionaries. He became a respected author. Locked up in 1961 for stealing seventy dollars in the armed robbery of a store, he received the original crazy as hell sentence of one year to life. While in prison he read Marx, Lenin, Trotsky, Engels, and Mao (google 'em if you don't know what they were writing about) and studied political economy. Yeah, he was in prison studying political economy. His two books, *Soledad Brother* and *Blood in My Eye*, are classics of the sixties. Jackson had a literary love affair with another *Crazy as Hell* shero, political activist Angela Davis, and through letters trained his younger brother Jonathan Jackson to operate as a revolutionary. (Jonathan also makes the *Crazy as Hell* list.) George Jackson is also one of the founders of the Black Guerrilla Family. When you think about George Jackson, ask yourself this question: How do you steal $70 and wind up a part of Black history? That sounds a little crazy, don't it?

Eldridge Cleaver

OUT OF ALL THE PEOPLE IN THIS BOOK, Eldridge Cleaver lets you know that no matter how crazy you are, you too can be a part of Black history. Though we include Cleaver here in the Inmates section, he also could be in a serial rapists category. Now imagine a convicted rapist who, in his bestselling book, admitted to raping Black women to prepare for assaulting white women and saw the *New York Times* rate his book as one of the "ten most notable" of the year. Eldridge Cleaver was a serial rapist, convicted felon, and member of the Black Panther Party. Later in his life, he became a Mormon (back when Mormon doctrine said Black folks could not get to heaven) and a Republican. We suggest you look him up, and to get you to do it, we'll add this one last fact: Cleaver, at one time, got into fashion design and created a codpiece he called "virility pants," which featured a bump that looked like a penis. We're not making this up. Seriously. Google it. Crazy as hell.

Reginald Dwayne Betts

THIS BROTHER COULD EXIST in this book in half a dozen categories, some that exist and some that don't: the Convict, the Negro Fabulist, the Superpredator (a term used by Hilary Clinton to argue more teenage Black boys needed prison instead of rehabilitation or love). He don't belong in none of them though; he's adored by every Aunty that he's ever met, and he confesses to some Black existential need to become crazy as hell to survive the way the memory of a slave ship in the Atlantic lingers. He almost been in two scuffles behind his take on *Crazy as Hell* alum Eldridge Cleaver. In brief: fuck that rapist. A prolific scholar whose felonious childhood would provide a narrative that would allow him to Segway into a lifetime of philanthropy, undaunted leadership, and literary excellence. Most recognized for his poetry, Betts would also find himself to be a master orator and highly recognized literary genius. His accomplishments and accolades would be considered astounding, as he would be viewed as a true visionary carrying his generation. Fool raised 20 million dollars to deliver to the place where he experienced so many nightmares. Betts has been known to go by at least a half a dozen names: Reginald, Reggie, Dwayne, Juice, Shahid, Shy, Shy Boogie, Rugged Child, Music, Young Music, Young, Betts. His middle name, Dwayne, was the first name he knew. Reginald or Reggie was immediately and unofficially abandoned by his family out of fear that his uttering his father's name would land him in prison or make him start smoking crack. Betts has avoided the latter, and some believe he turned himself in for a crime that didn't happen because he had a dream that only the deserved suffering of Black men makes them worthy of the tears they'll need to float through this world. A bookstore once hailed him the Patron Saint of Regrets, which would be the most relevant of titles. The father and husband lives somewhere between honor and vulnerability on more than one occasion in his lifetime, the last giving him his greatest label—triflin. They say he lost his virginity twice. A woman once said he reminded her of Andy

Dufresne. Rumor also has it that although he was a convicted felon, he was nonviolent. So nonviolent that he unknowingly came close to becoming a victim of a beige girl's plot to rob him for his fashions at an innocent age. Betts may be the luckiest felon who served time for a crime where the only one hurt was a woman who was nowhere near the scene for the catalyst to his legacies.

More on the Inmate

■ If you want to read about the prison industrial complex and the way Black people get caught up in it, check out Michelle Alexander's *The New Jim Crow: Mass Incarceration in the Age of Colorblindness* or Ava Duverney's documentary *13th.*

■ You should really check out Spike Lee's epic film *Malcolm X.*

■ Read George Jackson's 1960s classic prison books *Soledad Brother* and *Blood in My Eye.*

■ Read the poetry of Randall Horton and Reginald Dwayne Betts.

The Committed

THERE IS ANOTHER CATEGORY OF PEOPLE who get locked up for a stretch of time. And in those asylums they may not even be asked to work. In some ways, slavery is just a mental institution where you gotta work all day, and the folks in charge act like you crazy for saying you want to get paid or, at the very least, to rest your feet. The committed are imprisoned because either they're just plain crazy or completely forgot how to act. It's like they don't need to be free or can't even dream about freedom. Being committed is almost the same as being in prison; the difference is in prison, they repress your mind cuz you did a crime; in a mental institution, they say your mind isn't important cuz it don't work right.

So in our journey through Black history, we gotta spend time checking out those poor Black people who were called crazy and lost the power to run their own lives. It's inevitable that some people crack under the pressure of racism, but remember there must have been crazy people in Africa. Though it's hard to imagine, some of us probably came here crazy.

PUBLIC SERVICE ANNOUNCEMENT

In this context, the word *committed* means "being locked up in an asylum," but in another context, it means "to be completely dedicated to something or someone." So in one sense, nearly everyone we talk about in this book was *committed*, and maybe that is the most sane thing that you could be when things are going crazy. To be committed means there is no debate. You in prison. You locked up. But even these *committed* folks do beautiful things. We leave it to readers to decide if the *committed* Black genius is really crazy.

Buddy Bolden

THE LEGENDARY BUDDY BOLDEN was born Charles Joseph Bolden on September 6, 1877, in New Orleans, Louisiana. As leader of the most popular ragtime band in town, he became known as King Bolden. We don't know much about the man except that he was a tall, brown-skinned, handsome player whose cornet playing made him among the founding fathers of jazz. But you can't find video of his music on YouTube. He lived before they were making records, let alone videos. What's left of his music are stories passed down by people like King Oliver and Bunk Johnson, who played in his band. Even Jelly Roll Morton, who called himself the originator of New Orleans jazz, paid homage to Bolden in his "Buddy Bolden Blues." But in 1906, his mind began to go. Bolden was diagnosed with schizophrenia and completely forgot that he even played music. He was committed to East Louisiana State Hospital, where he died November 4, 1939.

Crownsville Hospital for the Negro Insane

THIS MENTAL HOSPITAL, located in a town in Maryland with the same name, is the inspiration for this book. Crownsville, built by African American patients with mental illnesses, operated from 1910 to 2004. During that time, patients cleaned tens of thousands of pieces of laundry like they were still enslaved. They were also subjected to lobotomies, wretched surgeries where doctors cut out a part of the brain in an attempt to cure mental illness.

The problem is that Black folks may be called crazy and get locked up because they are free thinkers. Not everybody is cut out for following rules that were, after all, often designed for the benefit of other people. Some people may find ways to externalize this conflict. Others might internalize it. It sounds crazy as hell, but the real problem with slavery is that we wanted to be free no matter what happened. Think about it: If the white people in America could have afforded it, they would have cut out the part of the brain that made African Americans want to be free.

While we still tell jokes about folks being crazy as hell, some of us really struggle with mental illness. Bipolar disorder and schizophrenia are common diagnoses that stand out because these two forms of mental illness suggest that the mind is somehow divided into two selves, which sounds a lot like the famous idea of "double consciousness" coined by one of America's most famous intellectuals, W. E. B. Du Bois, in his classic *The Souls of Black Folk*.

Louise Little

LOUISE LITTLE, THE MOTHER of *Crazy as Hell* hero Malcolm X, had it rough for at least two reasons. First off, she was born of a rape that occurred when her mother was only eleven years old. Next, her husband, Earl Little, was brutally murdered because he was an activist for social justice. After his death, she was left to raise ten children on her own. So naturally, eight years later in 1938, Louise Little was committed to the Kalamazoo State Mental Hospital. Malcolm turned to crime and drug use, partially because of his father's death and his mother's mental illness. It wasn't until 1963, just two years before Malcolm was assassinated, that he and his brothers and sisters secured her release from the mental hospital where she had resided for twenty-five years. No one talks much about the role her insanity must have played in making Malcolm Little into Malcolm X, but there's no way someone's mama can be committed and them not spending time thinking about what it is like to be crazy as hell.

Charlie (Bird) Parker

IN 1945, THE GREATEST JAZZ SAXOPHONIST to ever live was once committed to Camarillo State Mental Institution in California. These days, folks would say Charlie Parker was an addict. In those days, they said he was crazy. He was born August 29, 1920, and died in New York City March 12, 1955. He was nicknamed "Yardbird" or just "Bird" for short. Some folks said Bird played so well because he was high on heroin. Shortly after being released from the hospital, he recorded "Relaxin' at Camarillo," a song he wrote to go with his confinement. Imagine getting locked up for being crazy and then writing a song about it. That's a little crazy. Listen to some swing. Then listen to bebop. There's a lot of it on YouTube. How does a musician get from one to the other? Was Bird crazy as hell or a genius? It's a riddle of Black history. Are we smart or just crazy?

Nina Simone

BORN EUNICE KATHLEEN WAYMON in 1933, she made up the stage name Nina Simone to hide from her parents the fact that she was singing in an Atlantic City nightclub. She was never committed to an institution but some say she could have been. She was a classically trained pianist who took the singing job to pay for music lessons. The nightclub owner insisted that she sing while accompanying herself. So she started singing, and her career took off.

For a while, Simone lived next door to *Crazy as Hell* hero Malcolm X. Their children played together like neighbor children do. Although she is well-remembered for her moving tribute "Why? (The King of Love Is Dead)," first performed three days after the Rev. Dr. Martin Luther King, Jr.'s, assassination, rather than the nonviolent approach preached by King, Simone shared many of Malcolm's nationalist views, including the need for armed resistance.

Simone had all the attributes necessary for a lucrative career as a performing artist, with hit songs like "I Loves You, Porgy" and "My Baby Just Cares for Me," but she insisted on making songs like "Mississippi Goddam" and albums like *Young, Gifted, and Black*. Of course, her gigs dried up. Add to that the physical and psychological abuse both taken and given at home and you have a recipe for crazy. Check out the documentary on her called *What Happened, Miss Simone?* featuring her daughter and others if you want to learn more about her.

Lafargue Psychiatric Clinic

THE FAMOUS AUTHOR OF *Native Son*, Richard Wright co-founded the Lafargue Psychiatric Clinic in Harlem along with Dr. Fredric Wertham in 1946. It operated until 1959. You should google Dr. Wertham's approach to psychology. It was pretty hip. At a time when psychiatric services were reserved for wealthy white people, the clinic was democratic in its approach to mental health. Wright agreed with Dr. Wertham's approach and introduced him to another famous author, Ralph Ellison, and others who saw a link between the schizophrenia of the nation's policies and artistic production. Think of spirituals, the blues, jazz, bebop, soul, R&B, hip-hop—the list could go on to include nearly everything Black people ever made. Maybe we create such beautiful things because we gotta deal with the crazy in our lives?

The Lafargue Clinic was one of the first places in the country that actually treated Black people's mental health. Back then, folks was still running around thinking there were no Black serial killers and that Black people didn't kill themselves. Black folks wasn't even dreaming of therapy then. But the newspaper headline announcing the opening of the clinic read "They're Crazy Anyway." They wrote it that way because they didn't want to say "Niggers is Crazy Anyway." Maybe. Maybe not. We ain't here to argue about Black people not being crazy. The whole thing misses the critical point, which is that *racism* drives you crazy!

More on the Committed

- Watch *Bolden: Where the Music Began* (2019), a film directed by Dan Pritzker starring Gary Carr as Buddy Bolden.

- Dr. Fredric Wertham's papers are open to the public at the Library of Congress.

- Read the article by Whitney Balliett published February 23, 1976, called "Bird: The Brilliance of Charlie Parker" in the *New Yorker*.

- On the website aclu-md.org there's an article titled "Crownsville: A Piece of Maryland History That Shouldn't be Forgotten," written February 28, 2014.

- *What Happened, Miss Simone?* is a really interesting documentary about Nina Simone.

The Badass

EVERYBODY KNOWS SOMEBODY BLACK who never seems to stay in their place. Often this begins in the home, at the heart of the community. Bold Black folks never fit into the second-class status assigned to African Americans. They don't seem to hate themselves. They are bold—bold enough to do something other folks think is crazy. These Black folks are known for never backing down, standing their ground, and challenging the power held by white folks. On the right day, the right badass Black person will make you think they bulletproof. They'll fight the power, challenge racism, defend themselves, and live to tell about it. Badass can be like magic. Search for the examples; there is hope.

PUBLIC SERVICE ANNOUNCEMENT
Be careful about being bold. Given the dangerous nature of racism and the evil that sets the stage for much of Black history, we have to stress that there is a difference between badass and stupid. It's like the folks on TV who jump over cars and do stunts. If you have not studied with the right bold Black person, please do not scream at white folks, brandish weapons, back talk your boss, or do some stupid shit that will get you fired, locked up, or killed. These badass Black people are masters of their craft, legitimate Black history heroes who honed their skills through dangerous encounters. Show some respect. If you don't know what you are doing, leave this one alone.

Madam C. J. Walker

BORN ON A LOUISIANA COTTON PLANTATION in 1867 and orphaned at ten years old, Madam C. J. Walker would later claim that a big, Black man appeared in a dream one night and told her the recipe for a concoction that grew hair. That sounds a little crazy. Except Madam C. J. Walker became the first American self-made woman millionaire. The hair-growing formula was just the beginning of what would turn out to be an unprecedented organization of Black professionals who could make in a week what it would have taken them a month to make as domestic laborers. After another *Crazy as Hell* notable, Booker T. Washington, denied her a place on the agenda at the 1912 National Negro Business League convention, Walker took it upon herself to address the body anyway. She told them, "I am a woman who came from the cotton fields of the South. I was promoted from there to the washtub. Then I was promoted to the cook kitchen, and from there, I promoted myself into the business of manufacturing hair goods and preparations." By 1916, her company employed 20,000 agents across the United States, Central America, and the Caribbean.

Ida B. Wells-Barnett

YOU HAVE TO BE CRAZY to be a journalist committed to reporting on lynching with any honesty back when they was regularly stringing Black folks up. It was a dangerous job. Folks talk about freedom of the press, but lynchers murder. They were killing Black folks for less. It's crazy as hell to think somebody gonna give you freedom of speech when they won't even let your body be free. Ida B. Wells-Barnett gets the *Crazy as Hell* award for working toward freedom of speech when there was clearly no freedom of speech.

Think about it: Lynchings are state-sanctioned mob violence promoted with as much celebration within the white community as parades on the Fourth of July. When white people reported on lynchings, they wrote things like this quotation from *The Monticello News* following the murder of the Barber family in 1915: "It is needless to say that no one knew from whence the mob came and whither it went after the lynching was over." When Ida B. Wells-Barnett reported on lynching she wrote things like "A Winchester rifle should have a place of honor in every Black home, and it should be used for that protection which the law refuses to give." Even after they burned down her print shop and ran her out of town, she just kept writing about lynchings, drawing a link between racial oppression and exploitation and white economic opportunity. That's a wee bit crazy. Even crazier than that is the fact that she was posthumously awarded a Pulitzer Prize for journalism in 2020, the year of the COVID-19 pandemic and the global Black Lives Matter protests sparked by the murder of George Floyd.

Lou Ella Townsend

MOST PEOPLE HAVE NEVER HEARD of Lou Ella Townsend. They are more familiar with her daughter, the famed civil rights leader Fannie Lou Hamer. But Fannie Lou's mother may be the reason we got to know her to begin with. According to Charles Cobb, in *This Nonviolent Stuff'll Get You Killed*, folks in Sunflower County, Mississippi, knew that Townsend was one of them crazy Black people who could turn wild if pushed too far. He describes how Townsend would walk into the fields to work with a pan on her head and a bucket in each hand, one of them holding a cloth-covered 9mm Luger pistol. Once a white man rode up on Mrs. Townsend working in the fields with others nearby. Evidently unclear about how crazy she was, this man threatened to carry Townsend's niece off with him to beat her so she could learn her place. Mrs. Townsend informed him, "You don't have no Black children and you're not going to beat no Black children. If you step down off that horse, I'll go to Hell and back with you before Hell can scorch a feather." He left her and her niece alone.

Jim Evers

ANOTHER PERSON WHO WAS CALLED CRAZY by those who knew him well was Jim Evers, Medgar Evers's daddy. He didn't have a lot of formal schooling, but he could count good. So when he visited a general store one day with his sons, Medgar and Charles, and the manager tried to overcharge him, Mr. Evers refused to pay it. The manager got upset and threatened to kill him, heading toward a pistol behind the counter. Mr. Evers stepped between the manager and the gun, reached for a bottle of Coke, and smashed it on the counter to turn it into a knife. The other white men were like "He's crazy as hell!" and didn't even move. Mind you, this was in the 1930s and Mississippi. Mr. Evers directed his sons to walk out of the store. He followed without turning his back, and the three made it home alive. Even racist white store owners understood their limits when dealing with Crazy Jim.

Shirley Chisholm

BORN IN BROOKLYN, NEW YORK, in 1924. At four years old, Shirley Chisholm and her sisters were sent to live on her grandmother's farm in Barbados until she was ten years old. Chisholm returned home a solid student who would go to college and graduate school to prepare herself for a career in education. During this time, she became active in local politics through the Seventeenth Assembly District Democratic Club, where she learned that, even though women were the key leaders in fund-raising, their take on political matters were ignored. Chisholm was crazy enough to think that if Black women were good enough to raise money, then they were good enough to be heard. In 1968, in a move that we're going to assume inspired the titles of at least a thousand feminist anthems, this crazy woman, using the slogan "Unbought and Unbossed," became the first Black woman elected to Congress. She remained in the House of Representatives for fourteen years. But she is best known for her 1972 bid for the presidential nomination of the Democratic party.

Muhammad Ali

CASSIUS CLAY, LATER CALLED MUHAMMAD ALI, took his adopted name from a king of Egypt from the 1800s. Most people know Muhammad Ali as a lovable, trash-talking heavyweight boxer. But he put all that at risk. Muhammad Ali famously said, "I ain't got no quarrel with them Vietcong" (some claim he also said "Ain't no Vietcong called me a nigger," but that is probably apocryphal), justifying his refusal to fight in the Vietnam War. The statement sounds crazy as hell, especially coming from the heavyweight champion of the world. Many Black folks think similarly about American wars, but most of us are afraid to say it. Talk like that might end you up in prison, which is exactly what happened to Muhammad Ali. In 1967, after being stripped of his heavyweight title, Ali was sent to jail for refusing to comply with the draft. You should look up how much money he was making. He was on top of the world and went to jail cause he wouldn't sign up for the draft.

Jack Johnson

PRESIDENT DONALD TRUMP gave a posthumous presidential pardon to boxer Jack Johnson in 2018. Jack Johnson was the heavyweight boxing champion of the world in 1910 when he was convicted on charges that he violated the Mann Act, which was primarily a law used during segregation times to prosecute interracial couples. Johnson fled the country and spent years abroad appealing the case, but in 1920 Johnson returned and served a ten-month sentence at Leavenworth. Requests were sent to President Barack Obama by Senator John McCain and others. Obama denied them. It would have been crazy as hell for President Obama, the first African American president, to pardon a Black man convicted of a crime involving a white woman. [EDITOR'S NOTE: OR MAYBE IT WOULD HAVE BEEN A STEP TOWARD REPARATIONS, CONSIDERING HOW MANY BLACK MEN HAVE BEEN LYNCHED FOR ALLEGATIONS OF INVOLVEMENT WITH A WHITE WOMAN.]

But there's no doubt that Johnson was crazy. He was like High John the Conqueror. He knew how to fight, dated white women in the segregated South, and didn't back down from anybody. Folks say once, after being given a speeding ticket for $50, he tried to pay with a $100 bill; the officer said he didn't have change. Johnson told him to keep the change because he planned to speed on his way home too.

Single Mamas

THOUGH SINGLE MAMAS aren't just one person, we had to include them in *Crazy as Hell*. Trying to raise a child alone is enough to make you crazy. It starts off with sleepless nights and then goes through the terrible twos; you get a few honeymoon years when the kids are in elementary school, then bam! They hit you with the rebellious tweens and teens! Trying to raise a child alone can make you absolutely lose your mind! The idea of single mamas is so powerful that just seeing a Black woman pushing a baby stroller makes some of us imagine that there is no man in the child's life. If you google "Black single mothers," 2010 Census data says 72 percent of Black children are born to single mothers. More recent data collected by childtrends.org have a lower figure of 64 percent of Black children living in single-parent homes. Like the crack epidemic, no one really knows how it began. But at the risk of getting on white folks' nerves, here's our educated guess: We'd have to say it probably started in slavery when the Massa decided he was the father of everybody while at the same time making babies he didn't really parent. On top of that, there were children on the plantation whose fathers were on the auction block. Like *Crazy as Hell* Deadbeat Dads, stereotypes mix with truth, and Black families and marriages always seem to suffer. The thing is nobody is really a single mother. Black people still got families. People always help. And close to 60 percent of Black fathers live with their children (even if they are not married to the baby-mama).

More on the Badass

- You might be interested in this April 23, 2018, article by Ellen McGirt titled "Donald Trump, Colin Kaepernick, and Jack Johnson" on fortune.com.

- The National Archives has important holdings relating to Shirley Chisholm.

- Charles Cobb, Jr., writes a readable book called *This Nonviolent Stuff'll Get You Killed: How Guns Made the Civil Rights Movement Possible*, which should be in a library near you.

- Madam C. J. Walker can be found in the Guinness Book of World Records.

- Here's a good article called "Ida B Wells: the unsung heroine of the civil rights movement" on theguardian.com.

- Elizabeth Catlett's art often depicted badass Black women.

The Outlaw

SOMETIMES THE DIFFERENCE between an outlaw and an inmate is whether they have been caught. A pair of handcuffs turns many an outlaw into an inmate, but the outlaw's potential is increased by the sheer power to inspire folks by evading the Law. The original outlaw was the runaway slave. Somebody on your plantation breaks the law, everybody wants to break the law. A good outlaw inspires us to see unjust laws as unjust and to break the unjust laws. *Crazy as Hell* hero Martin Luther King, Jr., is like that.

You can choose whether you want to believe the outlaws' stories or not. Some of them sound like war stories, fools on the corner serving straight-up street talk, but the outlaw captures our hearts because we admire their fight and their flight.

PUBLIC SERVICE ANNOUNCEMENT

We know what you thinkin. It is part of the American tradition to view the outlaw as a hero. But please remember breaking the law is dangerous business. Our slave ancestors admired the law breakers who ran away, but they also had to deal with the sorrow that came when the runaway was caught, maimed, or punished. There's nothing more dangerous than breaking the law in a country where Black folks are perceived as symbols of criminality. Don't let Black history go to your head. Obey the law as much as you can, and if you choose not to, understand the risks and potential consequences. [EDITOR'S NOTE: CRAZY AS HELL, BUT RUMOR IS THAT THE EMANCIPATION PROCLAMATION HAS A SECRET CODICIL THAT PROVIDES MONEY FOR THE POLICE BRUTALITY LAWSUITS THAT WOULD INEVITABLY INCREASE AS SLAVERY ENDED, REPARATIONS BECAME A CONFEDERATE JOKE, AND DEATH AT THE HANDS OF THE POLICE BECAME A PATH TO GENERATIONAL WEALTH.]

Deacons for Defense and Justice

DEACONS FOR DEFENSE AND JUSTICE was incorporated on March 5, 1965, and, according to legend, the founders called themselves "Deacons" because most people only knew deacons from church. And you probably still don't know what a deacon ever does, besides commandeer the best pew. The Deacons for Defense and Justice decided if they called themselves that, no one would ever suspect that they would actually shoot white people in order to protect their own. They were created by the Congress of Racial Equality (CORE) in Jonesboro, Louisiana, for the express purpose of armed self-defense. I'd say look them up, but they weren't really trying to keep good records of their goings and comings. (There's a television movie based on them though.) They were a group of gun-toting Black men in the deepest of the deep South. You know they *had* to be crazy!

Assata Shakur

THERE ARE FEW HEROES in Black history like Joanne Chesimard, aka Assata Shakur. Assata Shakur is the play auntie of the late Tupac Shakur. She's also the subject of a song made by the artist Common. Like *Crazy as Hell* notable Mumia Abu-Jamal, she is one of Black America's most famous political prisoners. While most African American political prisoners remain in prison or were freed only after lengthy legal battles, Assata Shakur bears the distinction of being freed by her comrades in James Bond–like fashion from a maximum-security prison after being incarcerated for the murder of a New Jersey state trooper. Her famous *Assata: An Autobiography* gives no details of how she was broken out. Imagine escaping from a prison and spending the rest of your life on the FBI's most-wanted list? She has the spirit of the runaway and is still alive and well in Cuba. If you don't believe us, google her.

Jonathan Jackson

JONATHAN JACKSON WAS KILLED in 1971 after he went to the Marin County Courthouse carrying some guns owned by *Crazy as Hell* shero Angela Davis and took a federal judge hostage. Of course, he wound up dead. In the end, four people were dead: Jonathan, the judge, and two other prisoners who got involved once the mess started going down. He died at seventeen years old, like a soldier trying to get his brother and *Crazy as Hell* standout George Jackson out of jail. George was seen by many as a political prisoner, but soon he would be killed, too. No drugs were involved. Which means Jonathan had to be half crazy to imagine that he could take hostages and actually secure the release of his brother and other inmates from the Soledad prison. Or maybe he was just young.

More on the Outlaw

- Read Assata Shakur's *Assata: An Autobiography*.

- Listen to Common's "A Song for Assata."

- Bill Duke made a television drama in 2003 titled *Deacons for Defense*.

- You can find a bunch of scholarly articles on the Soledad Brothers that are worth reading if you search an academic library.

The Lawless

TO THE NOVICE STUDENT of Black history, the categories of Outlaw and Lawless may seem to be the same thing. The error is understandable. Both categories of craziness involve the law, but our approach to such matters is more detailed, more subtle. While the outlaw breaks the law, the lawless walk as if there is no law. Like the badass, the lawless seem bulletproof, but the difference is the lawless are bulletproof because they don't pay attention to danger. While the badass confronts danger, the lawless are oblivious to it. They do what we can't and appear to never suffer the consequences demanded of everyday Black folks.

PUBLIC SERVICE ANNOUNCEMENT
Even though we can make lawless folks seem the same kind of crazy that makes Black history noble, it is also important to say nobody wants to live in a neighborhood with lawless people. Sure, racism could drive you crazy, but complaining about racism while not paying child support or while unemployed is hard to sell. It's like you not handling business. Nobody wants to live in a neighborhood controlled by people who don't follow laws. Laws make life more orderly. Humans need that sense of security. People want to feel safe.

Rayful Edmonds III

RAYFUL EDMONDS IS THE OG OF OGS. By the time he was twenty-four years old, he made it into underground Black history because he was reportedly making $300 million per year selling crack cocaine up and down the East Coast. Edmonds made more money dealing crack than all the money African Americans spent buying books in the whole country. Folks bought more crack than books! That's crazy as hell! We romanticize those who flame young and sometimes burn out. Folks like Jay-Z glorified him in music, TV, and rap lyrics. But this was the late 1980s, and Edmonds' business-savvy drug dealing contributed to the decimation of Washington, DC. There were crack-heads, crack-babies, crack-houses. The murder rate rose to over 400 a year, peaking at 479 two years after Edmonds' arrest. Like so many heroes around the world with blood on their hands, many people still loved him. Most had no idea that he cut a deal with federal prosecutors as a snitch in exchange for a shorter sentence for his mother.

Bob Marley

THOUGH WEED IS LEGAL in many states now, most of us would not take as many pictures as Bob Marley did with a spliff in his mouth. He smoked so much weed, you could probably catch a contact high when he sneezed. It sounds crazy but as a Rastafarian, Marley smoked ganja as a sacrament. His band the Wailers became a spiritual icon for the world. Even folks who seem to hate drugs have some respect for his spiritual genius. Reggae was invented like jazz, blues, and the spirituals. Reggae is about love and resistance. In fact, Marley was descended from a special class of outlaws—the maroons, Black warriors who escaped from slavery, made it to the Jamaican mountains, and from that position waged war on the ruling classes. The reggae music they created became a symbol of freedom and abandonment for the whole world. One of his most iconic songs claims, "I Shot the Sheriff." We know that Marley didn't shoot anyone, but we love to sing his song, like we'd actually shoot a sheriff.

Robert Johnson

BEFORE DEALS WITH THE DEVIL became the property of cheap Hollywood flicks, folks say Robert Johnson met the Devil at the crossroads. (For those who don't know about the crossroads, look up the meaning of the crossroads in African cosmology. A lot happens at the crossroads.) Back in Africa, Papa Legba-Eshu guarded the crossroads. Papa Legba-Eshu is the courier god who totes messages between humans and the other gods. The crossroads is where they say Robert Johnson made a deal with the Devil that gave him the ability to play the guitar better than anyone else. For my money, that gamble is pretty crazy. But Johnson may well have come out ahead in the bargain since he sat for only two recording sessions and became a legend.

Nellie Jackson

FOR DECADES, NELLIE JACKSON KEPT a house of prostitutes in Natchez, Mississippi. She started as a bootlegger in the notorious Under the Hill slums before she moved to Rankin Street. According to three former mayors, everybody knew Miss Nellie Jackson's house was at 416 N. Rankin Street. She had Black sex workers, Vietnamese sex workers, German sex workers, Japanese sex workers, and white sex workers, but she only allowed white men as customers. (Watch the documentary about her called *Mississippi Madam: The Life of Nellie Jackson*.) This sounds crazy, but she was so much a part of the local scene that when a big-time federal official with the National Park Service was in town from Washington, DC, the members of the Mississippi Department of Archives and History's Historic Preservation Division brought him to Miss Nellie's house. It was late. They knocked on the back door. A young woman opened the door and asked what they wanted. They told her that they wanted to come in to have a beer and sit and talk. She told them, "Listen, we don't sell beer. We sell pussy. Now when you want some of that, you can come back."

More on the Lawless

- If you like crime shows, watch *American Gangster: Rayful Edmond III*, season 2 episode 9.

- *Mississippi Madam: The Life of Nellie Jackson* is a good documentary.

- Listen to *Robert Johnson at 100: Still Dispelling Myths* on npr.org.

- Or if you want to read a novel, Walter Mosley's *RL's Dream* is about Robert Johnson.

- Read about "The Life and Times of Bob Marley" in *Rolling Stone*, published March 10, 2005.

- Josephine Baker embodied a type of Black female lawlessness.

The Great Pretender

ONE OF THE HIGHEST LEVELS of craziness is espionage. Sometimes Black folks fake like they are something they are not. Naturally, this began with slavery. Black people had to act like good slaves to survive. Even after emancipation, Black people often found it necessary to cover their genuine intent with false pretenses. For instance, Black people pretended to believe that stuff about heaven and hell in the hereafter. Slavery left little doubt that they were already living in hell; they didn't have to guess who the Devil was. If a pig went missing around hungry slaves, they'd pretend to be confused about how they wound up eating barbeque.

Because this category involves trickery, even the sharpest students of Black history find it difficult to classify. You are required to see beyond deep contradictions and identify a Black person's true self. Is what looks like crazy really *crazy*? Is he just faking *crazy*? Or is she faking like she not crazy when she is *actually* crazy?

PUBLIC SERVICE ANNOUNCEMENT

If you pretend to be something all of the time, then you're not pretending. The risk is that a person becomes the thing that they started off pretending to be. The point of the mask is to protect the person that it covers, and often it protects the community, too. We all learned this during the coronavirus pandemic. But you have to take the mask off sometimes. If you can't ever take the mask off, then the mask no longer works the way it was intended to work.

Louis Armstrong

HERE IS A MAN who could stand up in the middle of the Jim Crow South during the civil rights era and play his horn and sing "What a Wonderful World." Maybe he was being ironic, but folks couldn't tell. Younger, less patient generations couldn't stand that about him. Ossie Davis among them. Ossie called it "Ooftah," that ability to sing and dance in a way designed to make the white folks happy. But Ossie changed his mind after he got to know the man better. One day, he happened upon Louis Armstrong in a quiet moment when he was sitting alone between performances. The look on Armstrong's face was so revealing that Ossie saw, for the first time, the man beneath the mask. He would later say of Armstrong that he had the power to kill within his horn. His opening and solo on "West End Blues" blew jazz wide open. There are a lot of recordings of his music. YouTube him.

Bill Cosby

BY THE 1980s, Bill Cosby had become a phenomenal salesman. He sold Pudding Pops. He sold out venues doing his comedy routines. He won six consecutive Grammys for best-selling albums based on those routines. Above all else, Cosby sold the image of himself as the Black version of father-knows-best. Cosby's performances catapulted him to universal acceptance. Who didn't love Heathcliff Huxtable, the character he played on *The Cosby Show*?

No kid who had called "Hey! Hey! Hey!" in the 1970s like they was hanging with Fat Albert and his gang or who wished they was one of them Cosby kids, would have believed that the man pretending to be Dr. Huxtable would spend time in jail. It's shocking to imagine the beloved TV celebrity, who represented Black middle-class values, as someone accused of multiple sexual assaults and rape. Just think of the irony, after teaching morality to Black folks, often suggesting poor Black people didn't educate their kids right or give them proper morals. Of course, Cosby denies all allegations against him and stands without a conviction.

The accusation is like the reverse of those made to justify so many lynchings—when white folks accused Black men of raping white women, then drove them out of town or made a public spectacle of killing them. The Tulsa race riots in 1921 were sparked by the alleged assault of a white woman. White residents responded by killing hundreds of Black folks and burning one of the wealthiest Black communities in the country to the ground.

It would be crazy as hell to continually rape women. But then again, one of our most beloved founding fathers, Thomas Jefferson, had both a wife and a slave "concubine," Sally Hemings. He fathered six children by Hemings, who was somewhere between the ages of fourteen and sixteen when he first had sex with her. That's right. The president of the United States had six children by a slave, and nobody calls it rape. Crazy as hell.

O. J. Simpson

O. J. SIMPSON'S RESUME IN BRIEF: The first professional running back to rush for more than 2,000 yards in a season, inducted into both the College Football Hall of Fame and the Professional Football Hall of Fame, and the first running back to score a touchdown while hocking rental cars in a TV commercial. Simpson retired from pro ball after eleven years before going into broadcasting, acting, and advertising.

Simpson had us riveted to our TV sets. At first on the field. Then leading the LAPD on a slow-speed chase. It's hard to reconcile the image of Simpson crouching in that white Ford Bronco with the memory of O. J. running the gridiron. After finding fame, Simpson largely turned his back on Black people, but when he was accused of murdering his ex-wife, Nicole Simpson, and her friend Ron Goldman he retreated into the comforting arms of the Black community. To mount his defense for what was called "the trial of the century," Simpson hired a powerful legal team led by the brilliant Johnny Cochran. Cochran's famous line, "If it don't fit, you must acquit," in reference to the blood-soaked leather glove that Simpson seemed to have difficulty putting on during the trial, clearly offered reasonable doubt because the jury acquitted him. Not saying that they did, but even if they thought that the LAPD framed a guilty man, Black people wouldn't care. They remembered the countless murderers who had walked free after killing Black people, like the men who killed Emmett Till and bragged about it in *Look* magazine. African Americans across the country celebrated the fact that Simpson beat the charges.

Although, in the eyes of many, he had gotten away with murder, that wasn't good enough for Simpson, because he's crazy as hell. On September 13, 2007, Simpson led a group of men into the Palace Station Hotel and Casino to take sports memorabilia at gunpoint! While he claimed he was merely retrieving stolen items, he was convicted of multiple felony counts and served nearly nine years in a Nevada prison.

Clarence Thomas

LIKE MANY HIGHLY SUCCESSFUL Black people, Clarence Thomas claims he was motivated by racism against his grandfather. He recalls a time when his grandfather came home very upset after being stopped by police for wearing too many clothes. We know there are rules against driving around butt naked, but can you imagine someone for real for real putting a law on the books about wearing too many clothes? Dealing with the enforcement of arbitrary and ridiculous rules makes you crazy—which is why the young Clarence Thomas remembers that his grandfather came home in the middle of the day after this incident and drank.

Most Black people can relate to stories like this, have similar stories that they could tell, yet we don't really like Clarence Thomas. He was born of Geechee-Gullah people in 1948, and his mother says he was too stubborn to cry. He was the only Black Supreme Court justice from 1991 to 2022. During his confirmation hearings, Anita Hill accused him of sexual harassment, sparking a media spectacle that Thomas called a "high-tech lynching." Regardless of her credibility, he was still confirmed. Given his wife's ongoing election denial following the election of Joe Biden and his enormous pile of ethics scandals, Thomas is a dubious character at best. The thing is, while the court is in session, the man hardly speaks. During one ten-year stretch he didn't ask a single question. He decided to engage more after the COVID-19 pandemic moved the Supreme Court to tele-conferencing in May 2020, but before that, the man had only spoken in about 32 of 2,400 cases since 1991. He wrote a book called *My Grandfather's Son: A Memoir*, and there's a documentary about him you can check out on PBS.

More on the Great Pretender

- Check out Kehinde Wiley's large-scale paintings of Black people on classical European backdrops.

- If you have the stomach for it, read Clarence Thomas's *My Grandfather's Son: A Memoir* and Bill Cosby's *Fatherhood*.

- Danny Hakim and Jo Becker wrote an article called "The Long Crusade of Clarence and Ginni Thomas" for the *New York Times Magazine*, February 22, 2022.

- History.com has "9 Things You May Not Know about Louis Armstrong."

- There are tons of things to watch on O. J. Simpson— documentaries, TV shows, and movies—and most of them include the most tawdry elements of his relationship with Nicole Brown Simpson.

The Wanderer

THE WANDERER IS MOST EASILY DISTINGUISHED from the Runaway by the speed at which they move as well as their motivation for moving. The wanderer moves more slowly because they are not running away from something. Also, their manner appears less deliberate. They travel like a monarch butterfly, purposefully yet subject to the winds. It is this quality of flightiness that makes wanderers seem crazy. They are not attached to people, places, and things in the way that most of us are. That is why when we encounter wanderers, we be thinking they crazy as hell. Folks are supposed to be trying to get somewhere.

PUBLIC SERVICE ANNOUNCEMENT
Wandering is like serendipity in that it opens up the possibility for happy accidents. If you allow yourself time to wander, either by walking around or driving aimlessly, or you let your mind wander through daydreams, then your chances for invention or encounters increase.

Medgar Evers

WE KNOW MEDGAR EVERS as the WWII veteran who became a civil rights activist before being shot and killed in the driveway of his home in Jackson, Mississippi, on June 12, 1963. His death sparked James Baldwin to write *Blues for Mister Charlie*. In fact, he's such an iconic figure that there's a college in Brooklyn named after him. His father, Jim Evers, is another of our *Crazy as Hell* legends included in this collection, which might suggest that crazy runs in families. As a boy while playing, Medgar Evers would sometimes issue a set of directives to his friends. They'd engage the game, only to find that Medgar had left them there playing while he wandered off. His mother sometimes found him under the house alone. When she asked him what he was doing under there, he'd tell her that he was thinking. Mrs. Evers shared this story with her daughter-in-law, Myrlie, when she seemed a bit flabbergasted by another of Medgar's disappearances.

Booker T. Washington

BOOKER T. WASHINGTON was the most powerful African American of his day. And he left an enduring legacy: the Tuskegee Institute, where he served as the founding president. Yet he came from humble beginnings, like most of our *Crazy as Hell* peeps. His life story is famously told in his memoir *Up from Slavery*. As he tells it, he boarded a train to start his five-hundred-mile journey from Maldon, West Virginia, to Hampton Institute, where he hoped to enroll, but after his ticket ran out, he walked the rest of the way. It is a little crazy to travel that far with no money and uncertain prospects of whether he was going to actually be admitted. But he got to Hampton and did so well that there's a life-sized sculpture of him on campus now. Folks give Washington a hard time because he told white people, in what is known as the Atlanta Compromise speech, that "In all things social we can be as separate as the fingers, yet one as the hand in all things essential to mutual progress." W. E. B. Du Bois, for one, wasn't having any of it. But perhaps we should allow for the possibility that old Booker T was playin us. He might have become the first Black man to eat dinner with a sitting president at the White House because he played like Br'er Rabbit. Think about that for a minute.

Huey P. Newton

THAT THE FOUNDER OF THE MOST ICONIC Black revolutionary group in America, the Black Panthers, died on the street after a crack deal gone bad is so sad it sounds like a made-up FBI story, but it's the recorded history. Huey P. Newton was born in 1942 and, in spite of his fame, and like a lot of other *Crazy as Hell* heroes, he died young—at the age of forty-seven. It seems that part of Black history is that *Crazy as Hell* heroes often die young. Tupac and Biggie in their twenties, Malcolm and Martin around forty. Huey's death from messing around with crack could depress even the most optimistic. Folks respected Newton as a thug, even though folks say he once sodomized Bobby Seale as a punishment for some offense. But he hung with a crazy crowd. Twenty-nine of Huey's comrades had the audacity to walk into the California State House in 1967 armed with shotguns and Magnum .357s to protest laws that worked against African Americans' access to Second Amendment rights. Who knows what he could have done if he had lived longer? (Take Trump, for instance: a crazy white man who was born in 1946, just a few years after Newton, and after bankruptcies, lewd comments to women, hanging with porn stars, and running reality TV shows, assumed the presidency at the age of seventy-one. Part of the main reason Trump got elected is folks thought that he would protect their Second Amendment rights.)

Amiri Baraka

AFTER THE DEATH OF MALCOLM X, LeRoi Jones changed his name to Amiri Baraka and changed the way he thought about white people. Up until then, he had written poems, plays, and had even married a white woman named Hettie Cohen. (In crazy as hell Black history, relationships with white women are important but also mysterious. Black history makes Black and white seem more important than they really are, and when it comes to attraction and sex this leads to many strange forms of human interactions.) Baraka divorced Hettie as he moved from white literary circles and became a major leader in the Black Power movement. And though he is unquestionably one of Black America's most brilliant minds, he was also once arrested for carrying an illegal weapon and resisting arrest during the 1967 riots in his home city of Newark. In August of 2002, he was selected as Poet Laureate of the State of New Jersey. When he read his poem "Somebody Blew Up America," it upset people so much that the state asked him to step down from the position. He's crazy as hell, so you know he refused. In the end, New Jersey abolished the position. You can google the poem and see what you think.

Bass Reeves

BASS REEVES WAS BORN INTO SLAVERY but escaped during the Civil War. He headed west, like many other African Americans. Eventually, Reeves, who was an excellent marksman and rode a silver horse, became a lawman. He traveled with a Native American friend. You have to be a little crazy to decide to be the po-po in the Wild Wild West. It's kinda inspiring, though. Maybe that is why they used him as inspiration for the iconic character the Lone Ranger. But Reeves wasn't really all that unusual. One in four cowboys was African American during the nineteenth century. In fact, "cowboys" was initially a derogatory name for the Black men who were given the roughest tasks on the frontier, like breaking horses or wading first into the river when driving cattle. That's another fact that's been buried over time. But it's true!

Bessie Coleman

BESSIE COLEMAN, the twelfth of thirteen children, was born on January 20, 1896, in Texas to Susan Coleman, who scraped out a living picking cotton. Each of her siblings joined their mother at around eight years old in the fields to help support the family. However, her mother made Bessie bookkeeper for the family rather than sending her to work the fields. Over the years, Bessie continued to find ways to avoid backbreaking work and finally left the South to join two of her brothers already living in Chicago.

In Chicago, she worked as a manicurist in the White Sox barbershop, where she heard stories told by vets returning from World War I. This is when Coleman got the crazy idea that she would fly. Coleman managed to get the support of wealthy Black philanthropists Robert Abbott, founder and editor of the *Chicago Defender*, and Jesse Binga, founder and president of the Binga State Bank, and left for France. Coleman studied aviation at the *Federation Aeronautique Internationale* and on June 15, 1921, received the first international pilot's license granted to an American aviator. So far, so good.

She became an accomplished aviator, topflight barnstormer, parachutist, and activist, capturing the attention of our own *Crazy as Hell* notable Ida B. Wells, who presided over her funeral when she died in 1926 at thirty-four years old after falling two thousand feet from a plane while rehearsing for an aerial show.

Peetie Wheatstraw

WILLIAM BUNCH WAS BORN IN RIPLEY, TENNESSEE, in 1902 and rose to fame as a blues performer who called himself "Peetie Wheatstraw, the Devil's Son-In-Law." Listen to the kind of stuff he'd sing:

I'm Peetie Wheatstraw, the High Sheriff from Hell.
The way I strut my stuff, oh, well, now you never can tell.

David Peel, a guy who studied his music, said, "Peetie Wheatstraw didn't come crying into the world like most of us; he was imagined by a man with a 'long head.' He wasn't born of a woman; he was thought up by a man who 'liked his liquor,' with the general idea of making both liquor and women easier to come by." It's no wonder that Ralph Ellison copped Peetie Wheatstraw for his novel *Invisible Man*. If you haven't read it, *Invisible Man* is a classic about an unnamed man who heads north to work after being expelled from school for showing an important white man the Wrong Kind of Black people. He hopes to do such a good job working in the north that he will be able to return to school. When he meets Peter Wheatstraw in Harlem, he is reminded of the Wrong Kind of Black people from back home—war vets who had been committed to an asylum for being crazy as hell.

More on the Wanderer

- Read Booker T. Washington's *Up from Slavery*; it's a classic.

- Check out the documents in the National Archives relating to Huey P. Newton.

- You can find information on Bessie Coleman on PBS's *American Experience*.

- Amiri Baraka (LeRoi Jones) wrote a really important book called *Blues People*.

- Printmaker Jacob Lawrence captures the Great Migration in his Migration Series.

- Colson Whitehead's Pulitzer Prize–winning novel, *The Underground Railroad*, takes an interesting approach to the historical timeline in a neo-slave narrative.

- Ishmael Reed's *Flight to Canada* is another neo-slave narrative that plays with time.

- You can find recordings of Peetie Wheatstraw's music on YouTube.

The Funky

BLACK PEOPLE DIDN'T FORGET EVERYTHING about who we were and where we came from when we came across the ocean in the Middle Passage. We spoke other languages, which meant we thought other thoughts. Those thoughts added the spice to the melting pot. This is why Black people can be so funky. You know some funky people. They the ones you love to go out to the club with—because when they're in the house, everyone has a good time. They dancing the new move, or they making a new sound, or they telling some wild story, or they creating some other new sort of art. We love them because they always bring the unexpected to the party. These funky folks right here are crazy as hell.

PUBLIC SERVICE ANNOUNCEMENT
You have to know the right beat in order to be funky. If you are not sure if you know the proper beat, start by listening to some African drummers. They always know the right beat. Then watch and see what your head and your feet do. If they do not bob and tap, then you probably do not have the proper gene. In that case, stand clear of dance floors and large outdoor gatherings where strangers are likely to upload videos of errant dance moves and make you the next victim on that Summer Jam screen.

Esther Jones

THE INSPIRATION FOR Max Fleischer's 1930 cartoon character Betty Boop was Esther Jones. Jones embodied the contradictions of sexuality and childishness. It's kinda crazy that she developed into a sex symbol by making herself seem like a child. As a regular performer in the famed Cotton Club during the 1920s, Jones donned the sensual dress of the flappers while making the girlish "Boop-boop-a-doop" into her signature sound and going by the name of "Baby Esther." After seeing Jones, Helen Kane adopted her style and even went so far as to sue Fleischer for stealing *her* likeness. Kane lost the case, however, when the court was presented with footage of Esther Jones performing. Of course, we still know of the character Betty Boop, and we may even remember Kane singing, "I wanna be loved by you . . . Boop-boop-a-doop," but the originator, Esther Jones, died in obscurity.

Parliament Funkadelic

THE GROUP STARTED IN THE 1950S AS THE PARLIAMENTS, singing doo-wop in barber shops. But after facing legal troubles regarding the use of the name, they pushed their band to the forefront and became known as P-Funk before finally landing as Parliament Funkadelic on a new record label in 1974. Talking about swimming underwater and not getting wet: Sounds like an African American Chinese proverb. Put that together with spandex, glasses, and glitter, and you know it's crazy as hell. Band leader George Clinton is so crazy that it was not out of character for him to come on stage naked at a banquet while folks were eating. But funk and rhythm don't lie. Clinton and Parliament Funkadelic are responsible for some of the most important African American classics of the seventies and eighties. When you get a chance to go to the National Museum of African American History and Culture, make sure you check out Parliament Funkadelic's mothership. They got it on display on the fifth floor.

Sun Ra

THOUGH HENRY SONNY BLOUNT was born in Alabama in 1914, he was always talking about space. His biography, *Space Is the Place*, discusses his strange journey as jazz musician, poet, and philosopher.

Members of Sun Ra's bands were known to yell out strange phrases at weird times, wear long robes, talk about Egypt, and play music that was, at times, pointless. Yeah, pointless. Sun Ra was into chaos as much as he was into swing. If you want to test your ability to understand the deep philosophy of his music, do a YouTube search. You can try "Space Is the Place," but there are many others.

Sun Ra and his group once marched into Central Park. Must've been like twenty people in the band. One of them walking on stilts. They were singing, "All we need to make the day is Ra, Sun Ra" to the tune of a children's nursery rhyme. After that they played a cut that sounded like all the noise in the world, followed by a perfect rendition of Duke Ellington's "In a Sentimental Mood." Right about now, you probably expecting us to tie what Sun Ra and his twenty did that day into some neatly packaged message—but that ain't what the funk's about. You just experience the funk. Then figure out what to do with it.

Kanye West

EVERYBODY KNOWS KANYE WEST is crazy as hell, but they also know he is the type of special that makes Black history so powerful and beautiful. What many folks don't know is West's mother, Donda West, was a distinguished literature professor before she stopped teaching to manage her son. Maybe we say he's crazy as hell because he married a white woman celebrity who has a very popular sex tape or because he is a Black man who met with and seemingly supported Donald Trump's 2016 bid for the presidency, or we could focus on his public references to being bipolar. A billionaire who speaks publicly about his struggles with mental health is a man made for history by anybody's standard. Think about this too: Kanye said "slavery was a choice." That's crazy as hell.

Michael Jackson

MICHAEL JACKSON SEEMED TO GET WHITER over the course of his life. This is both actual and metaphorical. Take a look at a picture of him when he was a little boy and compare it to the ones near his death. His nose is narrower from plastic surgery, and his face is at least four shades lighter. It don't seem fair to raise a kid to be a star like that. He can't help but turn out crazy.

He began as a child R&B singer and ended up transcending race and America as an international icon. All over the world, people love Michael Jackson. Always a boy at heart, many imagine he lost his childhood under the management of his crazy father, Joe Jackson. (Though Joe doesn't have an entry in *Crazy as Hell*, he sure could. In crazy as hell fashion, folks say he ran his family like a slave master ran a plantation.) But Jackson solved the problem of missing out on his childhood by creating the Neverland Ranch and Amusement Park in 1988 at the age of thirty. After purchasing the property for $19.5 million (Michael Jackson was also rich as hell), he named it after the mythical place in *Peter Pan*, the story about the boy who never grew up.

And look, we gotta bring up a delicate matter, at least delicate if you love *Off the Wall* like we do. People say MJ molested a rack of little kids at Neverland. We'll keep our comments on this for the barbershop. But to most of us, a grown man living in Neverland with obscene amounts of money and inviting children over for sleepovers seems crazy as hell. Then again, it's crazy as hell that people let their kids sleep over. If you don't believe us, go ask any Black mother if their child can have a sleepover at a man's house who is over thirty years old.

Flavor Flav

WILLIAM JONATHAN DRAYTON JR., known by the world as Flavor Flav, founded the hip-hop group Public Enemy with Chuck D in 1985, and they were already famous by the time filmmaker Spike Lee commissioned them to make the song "Fight the Power" for his movie *Do the Right Thing* in 1989. Flavor Flav became known for yelling "Yeeaaah boooyyeee!" and riling up the audience during performances. Hip-hop's tradition of the hype man is the playful part of the hood that makes it on stage. The world is about balance, and a Black man who wears a big ass clock around his neck is the perfect companion for Black folks talking seriously about fighting the power. Flavor Flav makes Public Enemy seem ridiculous and almost harmless. If you never saw one of his performances, google them so you know we ain't making it up.

Flavor Flav is the highest form of espionage Black folks can create. He is like the tricksters we talked about earlier, with a concealed weapon for self-defense and a radical Black consciousness. How we know? Chuck D once said Flav can play fifteen instruments. And we just believe it, because with Flav, anything could be true.

The problem is Flav got issues like most of us. Like many people in hip-hop, success did not keep him from crack cocaine and catching charges. It is hard to imagine, after time with Chuck D talking about radical changes in Black consciousness, one could actually use crack cocaine. But this is not unusual; Black and white celebrities be acting crazy as hell. And some of those who act like they crazy ain't just acting.

Erykah Badu

ERYKAH BADU'S WORK has received both commercial and critical success, because she's good, and because she's her own woman. During the coronavirus pandemic in 2020, before the Texas governor issued stay-at-home orders, the eccentric artist and vocal sensation showed up at the Texas Film Awards in a hazmat suit with Louis Vuitton logos spray-painted on it. That was a little extra. But that video she made ten years earlier was *extra* extra. On March 13, 2010, Badu shot the video for "Window Seat" while stripping naked on a busy public street. What's even crazier is the fact that the street she decided to walk down is the street where President John F. Kennedy was assassinated. She even had the nerve to end the video with the sound of a gunshot, her head snapping back, and her collapsing to the ground. She didn't get a permit for shooting the video, so they had to do it in one take. Walk down the street in the middle of the afternoon, where there are people of all ages, taking off one garment at a time, until finally Badu is butt naked, lying, as if dead, on the sidewalk. Get up. Then run like crazy. You can watch it online.

The Wu-Tang Clan

With special note of distinction for ODB

FOLKS REMEMBER THE FIRST TIME they heard the Wu-Tang Clan.
They formed in 1992 and released four gold and platinum studio
albums. The group was originally composed of rapper-producer RZA
and rappers Ol' Dirty Bastard (ODB), GZA, Method Man, Ghostface
Killah, Raekwon, Inspectah Deck, U-God, and Masta Killa. Probably
the most influential hip-hop group of all time. If you don't remember, you gotta listen to their stuff. The song "Method Man" don't
really make sense. But the Wu is the epitome of crazy as hell. A bunch
of folks from Staten Island singing in strange patterns about Chinese
kung fu flicks, street hustles, and the deep nature of Black culture?
Really, what does it take for a bunch of Black kids to name themselves
after a Taoist school of martial arts? (Taoism is a Chinese philosophy advocating humility and balance, based on the sixth-century
writings of Lao-Tzu.) The Wu-Tang's core philosopher, RZA, wrote
a book called *The Tao of Wu*. For those who don't know, tao can be
translated here as "the way." Think about that: Black rappers writing
books on and practicing Chinese philosophy. And as for ODB, his
run-ins with law as well as the crazy sound of his voice demand that
he be in *Crazy as Hell*. Or maybe ODB picking up child support checks
in a limo is all the reason needed for the entire Wu to make this list.

More on the Funky

- Jean-Michel Basquiat is one of the funkiest visual artists there ever was.

- DC native Chuck Brown's "It Don't Mean a Thing—If It Don't Got the Go Go Swing" is pretty funky.

- PBS claims to know "How James Brown Created Funk" on *Sound Field*.

- Folks even make pages on Pinterest about funk.

- New Orleans is pretty funky too. Check out Mardi Gras and the jazz funeral second line tradition.

- If you want to read something on the subject, check out Alexander Stewart's *Make It Funky: Fela Kuti, James Brown and the Invention of Afrobeat*.

The Serial Killer

FEW THINGS EVOKE AS MUCH FEAR AND LOATHING as a serial killer. Killing one person is bad. A pattern of killing is horrific. The serial killer is a nightmare that we make movies about. But they're as real as any of these other categories we've been talking about. The FBI defines a serial killer as a person who murders at least three people over the span of at least a month with an emotional cooldown period between the killings. When we were slaves, African Americans didn't usually run around killing people. Since then, Black people started killing for reasons similar to other people—over a jilted lover, or over some money, or because someone got high on some bad supply, or because Uncle Sam or the po-po commissioned them to do it. But serial killers murder for the thrill. Most Americans think of serial killers as white men, but some Black folks do it too. That's the kind of straight-up crazy person who should wind up in jail.

PUBLIC SERVICE ANNOUNCEMENT
These people are dangerous. On the rare chance that you encounter one of these, do not hesitate to call the authorities. In such cases, be clear: The police are not the enemy. The serial killer is— even if he or she happens to be Black.

Samuel Little

TRADITIONALLY, AFRICAN AMERICANS brag that Black people do not suffer from some of the mental illnesses commonly found among white people. For instance, Black folks told each other "Black people don't commit suicide" and "serial killers ain't Black." Taught it to our children like we taught them to rub Vaseline on their knees or to cook red meat until it's well done. Unfortunately, the fact of the matter is that Black people are subject to any of the pathologies found in white communities, and that includes sociopaths. In fact! The man acknowledged to be the most prolific serial killer in the country's history is a Black man named Samuel Little. And he lived long enough to get old. At seventy-nine, while in the custody of the Los Angeles County Prison, he confessed that, as he traveled across the country over the course of decades, he strangled ninety-three vulnerable women. Yeah. He's one of ours. And he's crazy as hell.

Wayne Williams

PERHAPS THE PRIMARY REASON the idea that Black people do not commit serial killings lasted so long is because victims of African American serial killers tended to be from the hood. The disappearance of a sex worker or a user doesn't upset the police. They act like it's one less criminal for them to worry about. It wasn't until 1979 or 1980 when thirty Black children—between the ages of seven and seventeen, with the exception of two young adults—began turning up dead in Atlanta, Georgia, that the country began to grapple with the likelihood of a Black serial killer. Wayne Williams was convicted of murdering two adults and was tied to, but never convicted of, the murders of twenty-two more victims. But the murders seemed to stop after he was incarcerated. Some folks don't think he did it, though. Forty years later, Atlanta mayor Keisha Lance Bottoms reopened the case in an effort to find more conclusive evidence.

John Allen Muhammad and Lee Boyd Malvo

ONE OF THE MOST INFAMOUS SERIAL KILLERS was known as the DC sniper. John Allen Muhammad terrorized the nation in his cross-country shooting spree in 2002. They say Muhammad became a serial killer to kill his wife. Yeah, he killed random people and then planned to throw his wife in at the end so folks would be like, "Some other random serial killer got her." Yeah. Crazy as hell.

Muhammad trained Malvo, who was a teenager at the time, to become a murderer too. Over time, the pair would commit hundreds of crimes, from robbery to assault, and they would shoot at least eleven people before their twenty-one-day rampage in October, when they ambushed thirteen random people, including a kid outside his middle school in Bowie, Maryland.

It took the police so long to catch them because everybody thought serial killers were white. Plus they were talking about the killer driving a white van. Maybe Muhammad was like the Spook Who Sat By the Door. Trained as an army sniper, he learned his trade as an employee of the U.S. government. Maybe the army taught him how to punch the keyhole out of the trunk of a car, pull out the back seat, and lay low so that he could shoot people. Or maybe he came up with that plan all by himself because he's just crazy as hell.

Christopher Dorner

THOUGH CHRISTOPHER DORNER SHOWS UP in the "serial killer" section, he challenges the category. Without a doubt, Christopher murdered people. But he was not a born killer. [EDITOR'S NOTE: I MEAN, IT'S NOT LIKE ANYBODY IS BORN A KILLER.] Dorner's case feels different than the other folks in this category. He was set off after he was fired from his job working as an LAPD officer for supposedly creating a false complaint that suggested an officer used excessive force when arresting a mentally ill man. Given what we know about police brutality in this country, it seems highly unlikely that he was lying. A disproportionate amount of police killings and brutality cases occur with the mentally ill. The mentally ill have more difficulty learning the proper postures when confronted by racists. So they pay higher tolls. Dormer noticed and attempted to implement protections. After being fired for trying to do right, like many of us, Dorner became perplexed by the wrong in the world. He simply couldn't believe he had told the truth and was punished for it. In the spirit of *Crazy as Hell* luminary Nat Turner, Dorner waged a short war on members of the LAPD and those connected to his case for nine days until he was later caught and killed.

More on
the Serial Killer

- In 2014, John White published a study of African American serial killers in the *Journal of Ethnicity in Criminal Justice* that is worth a look.

- Another scholar named Anthony Walsh published an article in *Homocide Studies* in 2005 called "African Americans and Serial Killings in the Media: The Myth and the Reality."

- Read Mackenzie Samet and Jackie Salo's article "New profile of serial killers debunks long-held myths," in the *New York Post*, August 14, 2018.

- Another interesting story is written by Wesley Lowery, Hannah Knowles, and Mark Berman called "Indifferent Justice: How America's deadliest serial killer went undetected," in the *Washington Post*, November 30, 2020.

The Spiritualist

THE SPIRITUALIST IS THE OPPOSITE of the serial killer. If the serial killer is addicted to extinguishing life, the spiritualist is compelled to perfect the energy that balances life. They see things that other people do not see, and for that reason, they do things that other people would not do, like fast for extended periods of time, or deny themselves some cherished pleasure, or use natural forces toward their own ends. Although the spiritualist believes in life, they often die young, leaving their work unfinished. They seem crazy to us because, while living in the visible world, they sacrifice so much for invisible gain. Really, folks gotta eat!

PUBLIC SERVICE ANNOUNCEMENT
Spiritualists are intensely charismatic but also often prone to isolation. Talk of the spiritual is far easier than actually living that way. If you meet a spiritualist, you might not even know them. They are the opposite of the megachurch preacher. There are many among us. Search for them in your circle. You will surely benefit.

Sojourner Truth

ISABELLA BOMEFREE WAS ONE OF THOSE crazy as hell folks who set out on a mission after hearing the voice of God. So she changed her name to Sojourner Truth and became a wandering preacher. For a time in her thirties, Truth lived in a commune. She left after the commune fell apart due to a free-love scandal and the fact that its founder, the self-proclaimed prophet Robert Matthews, was accused of murder, which may be about the only thing you can expect to happen on a commune led by a self-proclaimed prophet who declares that sex is free. Later, Truth and other people made silk while living and working together in a utopian community that didn't believe in dividing folks by race.

Along with Harriet Tubman, Truth is one of the best-remembered African American women of the nineteenth century. She became legend for her "Ain't I a Woman" speech presented in Akron, Ohio, in 1851 and for another given in 1858 during which she famously ripped open her shirt Janet Jackson/Justin Timberlake style to bare her breast before a disbelieving audience of primarily men who declared her speeches as too forceful to have been delivered by a woman. She was all like "If I am a man, then why do I have *these*?" But she also claimed to have been enslaved for forty years and to have lost thirteen children to slavery. The thing is, she only gave birth to five children, one of whom *was* illegally sold into slavery in Alabama. However, Truth successfully sued through the court in Kingston, New York, for his return. Can you imagine? She is one of the only Black women in the nineteenth century to use the legal system to win her son back from slavery. She knew better than to tell that story—she wasn't that crazy!

Marie Laveau

MARIE LAVEAU MARRIED JACQUES PARIS in 1819. She didn't kill
him. And he didn't die. So why does it matter? Marie Laveau did
what women did not tend to do in 1819. She told folks she was a
widow and went to live with Christophe Glapion. They went on to
have fifteen children. Laveau reigned as the high voodoo priestess
of New Orleans for at least forty years. She walked into the house
of a quadroon woman named Rosalie and stole a potent fetish that
had been carved in Africa from a tree trunk into a nearly life-sized
doll. Rosalie was the only person who came close to rivaling Laveau's
authority. That meant Laveau possessed the African fetish as well
as a magic shawl sent to her in 1830 from the emperor of China.
Imagine a Black woman in Louisiana telling you that the emperor of
China sent her a gift. Sounds crazy, don't it? But let me tell you something else, crazy be contradicting. Rumor is that Marie had at least a
handful of slaves during her lifetime. They also say that she slipped
poison to prisoners sentenced to death before their bid before the
gallows. Her daughter, also named Marie Laveau, became the second
voodoo queen, and you can still visit her house on Bourbon Street
in New Orleans.

Daddy Grace

YOU HEAR ABOUT MEGACHURCHES and pastors who act like pimps? Well, Charles Manuel "Sweet Daddy" Grace was probably the country's first celebrity preacher. He painted his ridiculously long fingernails in bright colors, grew his hair to his shoulders like Jesus, and dressed like Little Richard—*before* Little Richard. He traveled the country in the 1920s and 1930s, calling himself a "Bishop" and preaching to integrated audiences. He established the United House of Prayer for All Peoples. Daddy Grace grew obscenely wealthy off his followers. He preached that God only appointed one person at a time. He maintained, "Salvation is by Grace only. Grace has given God a vacation, so don't worry about Him. If you sin against God, Grace can save you. If you sin against Grace, God can't save you." Yeah. Absolutely insane! Look him up and see how much stuff he got off the peoples.

Elijah Muhammad

BORN IN 1897 IN SANDERSVILLE, GEORGIA, Elijah Muhammad would become the charismatic leader of the Nation of Islam from 1934 until his death in 1975. If you are familiar with *Crazy as Hell* hero Malcolm X or Minister Louis Farrakhan, you know something about Elijah Muhammad. He was sharp, yet most Black folks today think he was undoubtedly crazy. But in classic Black history fashion, a lot of us still know his name. Elijah Muhammad makes the *Crazy as Hell* hall of fame because he taught us to reject any spiritualism that treated us like dirt. Elijah Muhammad sent Malcolm X five dollars while he was still in prison and appeared to him in a vision. How many people you know sent money to a Black person in prison who wasn't related to them? Folks think he's a problem for society, but Muhammad taught his followers to obey all laws except conscription. That's the one that got *Crazy as Hell* hero Muhammad Ali locked up. Ali was a follower of Muhammad during the time of the draft for the Vietnam War. He also taught his followers to wear suits and bow ties and to call the white man the Devil, which sounds crazy.

Gullah Jack

GULLAH JACK WAS INVINCIBLE. At least that is what people thought. That is why he was so effective at recruiting people to join the *Crazy as Hell* legend Denmark Vesey's cause. One time when the conspirators met, Gullah Jack put a chicken on a table and performed a ritual over it. When he got finished, the plotters scrambled to get a piece of the chicken. Gullah Jack promised that they would pull the buckra apart just like they had pulled apart the chicken. Of course, there were snitches and bad weather, and ultimately it was the revolt that fell apart like the chicken. Turns out Gullah Jack was crazy as hell and before his time. He was the first to be executed in 1822, decades before the Civil War and after the verdict was handed down against Denmark Vesey and his co-conspirators.

John Africa

IN THE TRUE SPIRIT OF BLACK HISTORY, John Africa rose to national prominence because he died violently at the hands of officials. But his death is important because we learned that post-integration Black representation in high offices didn't necessarily change the outcomes. When you buck the system, you probably gon pay a high price. And John Africa bucked the system.

Truth is, though, we understand more about how John Africa died than we may ever understand about how he lived. Africa was the enigmatic leader of an organization based in the heart of a residential neighborhood in Philadelphia. The organization was known as MOVE, an anti-establishment, militaristic, naturalist organization. Their unorthodox lifestyle set them apart from their neighbors. Their children ran around naked with big bellies like those malnourished children in commercials that plead with us to feed the hungry. They built a bunker on the roof of their row home on Osage Avenue and blasted obscenity-laced messages from loudspeakers all hours of the day and night. Their neighbors thought John Africa and his crew were crazy as hell.

But if Africa was crazy, then he wasn't alone, because to evict MOVE from their home, someone authorized law enforcement agents to drop a bomb. Moreover, the police commissioner and fire commissioner's devastating decision to not put out the resulting fire occurred on Wilson Goode's watch. Goode happened to be the first African American mayor in the history of the city. That fire killed eleven people, five of them children. Unbelievable. They dropped a bomb on a house in the middle of a neighborhood and then burned down the entire block. You know it was a Black neighborhood. Check out Jason Osdur's documentary *Let the Fire Burn*. But stock up on tissue before you watch it.

Martin L. King, Jr.

MOST FOLKS KNOW the Rev. Dr. Martin Luther King, Jr., because his doctrine of love ushered in the modern civil rights era. The whole idea of turning the other cheek seemed crazy to a lot of people. Yet given the fact that there were all those cameras watching grown-ass white people brutalize Black kids, the nonviolent tactic worked pretty well. Kids played a huge part in the success of the movement. But when Dr. King was a kid, he tried to kill himself. At the age of twelve after the death of his grandmother, the man who would later become one of America's greatest symbols of freedom and justice jumped from the second story of his house, attempting suicide. (So much for all those years of Black folks insisting that we don't try to kill ourselves like other people do.)

Thankfully, his attempt was unsuccessful, but the man still seemed to have a death wish. Near the end of his life Dr. King chain smoked and is reported to have had numerous affairs. What's even crazier, when King received the Nobel Prize in 1964 with a cash value of $54,600 dollars (during a time when you could buy plenty of houses for much less than that), he donated all the money to civil rights organizations. By January of 1967, King moved with his wife and children into a $90-a-month flat on the top floor of a Chicago slum. He won $54,000, gave it all away, and then, four years later, moved into a cold Chicago slum with his wife and children. The front door didn't even have a lock! A man who spent his life trying to secure the safety of Black people everywhere couldn't afford to lock his own door. That's crazy as hell.

John Coltrane

JOHN COLTRANE WAS A LEGENDARY jazz saxophone player. Folks called him "Trane." Trane was born close to the railroad tracks in Hamlet, North Carolina, just like some of your grandparents. When he got a little older, he spent a short time in the navy. Like many vets, he got addicted to heroin. Unlike many vets, one day Trane quit cold turkey. He went on to play with some of the greatest jazz musicians of all time. There's a famous story of Trane playing with another of our *Crazy as Hell* luminaries, Miles Davis. As the legend goes, Miles confronted Trane about his extra-long solos. Trane told Miles that he was operating on impulse. He said, "I don't know what it is. It seems like when I get going I can't stop." Most of us don't listen to Indian music, but Coltrane did back in the late fifties and early sixties. If you want to get a sense of how crazy he is, google "Father, Son, and the Holy Ghost" or "Om," named after one of the principal sounds in the Hindu religion. If you can listen to all twenty-eight minutes of it, you may be crazy as hell too.

More on the Spiritualist

■ It might be hard to find Jason Osdur's documentary on the 1985 bombing of MOVE called *Let the Fire Burn,* but it is well worth watching.

■ Read the *I Ching*, the ancient Chinese Book of Changes

■ And the Holy Bible

■ And the Quran

■ And the Dao De Jing by Lao Tzu

■ And the Dhammapada

■ The Dalai Lama and Bishop Desmond Tutu co-authored *The Book of Joy: Lasting Happiness in a Changing World.*

The Angry

PROBABLY EVERY PERSON documented in this book could be indicted for their anger. How else does one decide to revolt or invent jazz or run away if they weren't angrier than most of the people around them? Anger is probably at the root of nearly every exceptional thing Black people ever did. On some level, people know this. They be quoting James Baldwin: "To be a Negro in this country and to be relatively conscious is to be in a rage almost all the time." But then turn around when folks act rageful, and be like something is wrong with them! If you get angry, you're supposed to act like you ain't angry. The folks included in this section are people who were unable to hide their anger.

PUBLIC SERVICE ANNOUNCEMENT
The thing about anger is, folks act like no one has a right to be angry. A little anger is all right; too much might eat you up. This is the most common of the Crazies. Most of us probably got anger issues. After all, we *are* Black in America.

Stagger Lee

IS THE QUINTESSENTIAL BAD MAN. The real Stagger Lee (aka Stagolee, Stag O. Lee, Stack O' Lee, and others) was a pimp named Shelton Lee who shot William Lyons in Bill Curtis's St. Louis, Missouri, saloon on December 27, 1895. Since before the turn of the twentieth century, musicians like Duke Ellington, Woodie Guthrie, James Brown, Bob Dylan, The Grateful Dead, Amy Winehouse, and, most famously, Lloyd Price have preserved the legend of Stagger Lee through song. In the musical version, the murder resulted from a dispute over gambling, which you could almost think reasonable. But really, the two men were drinking together when they began to argue over politics. Amid the heated exchange, Lyons took Lee's Stetson hat. Stagger Lee wasn't having it, and he pulled his .44 and shot Lyons in the gut. Stagger Lee was so crazy that he simply took back his hat and coolly walked away. Of course, Lee didn't get away with murder—he was a Black man who killed someone in front of witnesses. He was convicted and served time. And maybe he was still angry. After he was paroled, he assaulted someone else and got locked back up again, where he remained until his death in 1911.

Miles Davis

BY ALL ACCOUNTS, Miles Davis was a musical genius and a very angry man. Born May 26, 1926, Davis grew up in an affluent home in St. Louis, Illinois. His father was a successful dental surgeon and reportedly was the second wealthiest man in Illinois. But it was still the time of Jim Crow, and they were Black in America. Throughout his childhood, Davis's parents were at each other's throats. He didn't seem to draw a connection between his parents' violence and the violence in his own life. That's crazy as hell. One time, Davis refused to move along when directed by a white police officer. He was taking a break outside a club where he was headlining. The officer cared as much about Davis being a famed jazz musician as the people in Illinois cared about his daddy being the state's second wealthiest man. The policeman beat him bloody before hauling him off to the station. Davis had fistfights with club owners and cussed out fans. He knocked out his second wife at her mere mention that Quincy Jones was handsome. Cicely Tyson said after divorcing him, he remained her one great love. Another of his former wives said meeting him was like being in a movie and meeting a vampire, but you didn't care. After all, he was the birth of cool. That's the name of a documentary about him—*Miles Davis: Birth of the Cool*, which came out in 2019. You should check it out.

Mike Tyson

BORN JUNE 30, 1966, Mike Tyson became the youngest heavyweight boxing champion ever in 1986 at the age of twenty. He was strong, with quick fists and a formidable defense. People loved him. Fans would get together around a TV tuned to pay-per-view to watch one of his fights, and it would be over before they could get the cap off their beer. Tyson knocked out so many people in the first or second round that he earned the moniker "Iron Mike." Tyson won fifty of the fifty-eight professional matches he fought—forty-four by knock-out. But he was crazy as hell. After being convicted of raping a Miss Black America contestant in July 1991, he served time in prison. His brief marriage to Robin Givens was marred by accusations of domestic violence. And if that wasn't enough, on June 28, 1997, during a championship bout, all Gabriel Prosser style, he bit off a piece of Evander Holyfield's right ear! Like all crazy as hell folks, Tyson is a complicated dude. If you don't believe us, check out *Mike Tyson Mysteries*, where a cartoon version of him rolls up in a van like the A-Team meets Scooby Doo. Instead of solving crimes, though, his crew—a pigeon, a gay ghost, and his Chinese daughter—be making things worse. It's funny! Or check out his podcast, *Hotboxin' with Mike Tyson*, where the man who once knocked men out for a living is the insightful Unc that young cats smoke weed with and get game. It's funny!

More on the Angry

- We kinda all knew after watching the 1988 interview with Mike Tyson and then wife Robin Givens that their marriage wasn't going to end well. It's on YouTube. But if you want a laugh, check out *Mike Tyson Mysteries*. It's a delightful cartoon.

- You just need to listen to Miles Davis's *Birth of the Cool*. And then you can read Quincy Troupe's book called *Miles and Me*.

- This is classic: William H. Grier and Price M. Cobbs, *Black Rage: Two Black Psychiatrists Reveal the Full Dimensions of the Inner Conflicts and the Desperation of Black Life in the United States.*

- In 1961, in response to a question about being Black in America by a radio host, James Baldwin famously responded, "To be a Negro in this country and relatively conscious is to be in a state of rage almost, almost all of the time." Search NPR's website, where you can hear more.

The Black Intellectual and the Activist

IT TAKES A LOT OF CRAZY to be a Black intellectual. Think about it. Not long after our ancestors got here, we were banned by law from reading. Reading is brain work. Slaves were not supposed to *have* brains. Being a smart nigger could get you killed. So there's something noble about imagining that you could be smart, despite the fact that you or your ancestors were enslaved.

Activism is the same way. The original activists were fugitives running away to free themselves. Running could get you killed, and although we love the runaway, the majority of us did not run. Like we love books, while the majority of us don't read. (Not you, of course, because you are reading this book.)

But even most readers don't always understand what really smart people are talking about. Take someone like Cornel West, for instance. He's an intellectual who's written more than a dozen books. He's also got this crazy-looking Frederick Douglass Afro, which may or may not have anything to do with the subject of this book. Everyone who listens to him talk knows he is smart as hell, yet half the time we don't know what he's saying. That's the way it is with intellectuals. The other thing about Black intellectuals and activists is the way they seem to know more about white folks than the rest of us. We count on them to mediate for us, like Eshu-Legba moving between humans and gods, because they believe in the importance of white people *way* more than the rest of us.

PUBLIC SERVICE ANNOUNCEMENT
Contrast the intellectual with *Crazy as Hell* hero Malcolm X. Malcolm was crazy enough to use a microphone to say what many of us were thinking but too afraid to say. The intellectual is the opposite. They say things we would never think. Black Intellectuals and Activists today get paid to be smart and Black. They talk good and we hope their beautiful words will help to make us free.

Zora Neale Hurston

FOR A LONG TIME, people didn't know when Zora Neale Hurston was born. She was born January 7, 1891, in Notasulga, Alabama, but she told folks a lot of different years. Maybe because she was vain as many of her early biographers suggested; or maybe because both of her parents had been enslaved and her mother died young; or maybe because by the time she made her way to school, she had to lie about her age to be a student. And while Zora ended up being recognized as one of the greatest Harlem Renaissance authors, that ain't happen until after she'd died in poverty and had been buried in a pauper's grave.

Hurston and Langston Hughes worked together writing a play called *Mule Bone*. But the collaboration led to an argument which came to a head when Hurston showed up at Hughes's mama's house in Cleveland. But we ain't gonna call her crazy as hell for that. Sometimes you gotta show up at somebody's mama house. Still, the confrontation was so uncomfortable that Hughes asked Harlem's resident "white" friend Carl Van Vechten if *he* thought she was crazy.

And maybe she was, cause she literally made her work the collecting and telling of stories of Black folks. Best known for her novel *Their Eyes Were Watching God*, Hurston might have penned the most heartbreaking love story featuring a hurricane. It's a story of Hurricane Katrina before Katrina. You might have read it before; if you haven't, you might want to pick up a copy.

As a writer and anthropologist, Hurston was unapologetically rooted in her southern Black culture. Her practice of African religions and her strongly held independent beliefs led to her reputation for being undisciplined and eccentric, which is just another way of saying crazy. Hurston would walk up to strangers in Harlem if she thought they had an interesting head and measure it.

Nella Larsen

WHILE RECOGNIZED AS a Harlem Renaissance writer, for most of her life Nella Larsen felt alone. Born in Chicago on April 13, 1891, to a Danish mother and a West Indian father, who died when she was just two years old, Larsen felt like an outcast within her own family, which could make anyone feel crazy. Her mother remarried a white man, and together they had another daughter. Even though Larsen herself could have passed for white, she is recognized as the first Black woman to win a Guggenheim. It's crazy as hell that the very subject that made her a dope writer—that tension around who Black can become American—might have led her to borrow a story that wasn't hers to begin with. They say before heading to Europe to work on her third novel, Larsen seemed to lose it. She was accused of plagiarism, and although folks kinda supported her, even Larsen's version of events seems a bit shrouded. Larsen was a nurse, and she says that she drew the story from a patient who told her that her husband had been killed by a young Black man, and rather than report him to the white police, she decided to handle the young man on her own. Turns out, someone else had published a very similar account. And, according to a Black sociologist who was a friend of Larsen, "There are literally hundreds of these stories." Add to the stress of having to defend oneself against the accusation of passing someone else's story as her own, her marriage was floundering. Her husband had fallen in love with another woman. Larsen never seemed to fully recover and retreated into the relative anonymity of a career in nursing. Public spotlights are often enough to push folks to the edge. Thankfully, we still have her writing. You should check it out. Her stories are short, and you can usually find them published together as one book.

Angela Davis

ANGELA DAVIS IS CONNECTED TO two of our other *Crazy as Hell* heroes: George Jackson and his younger brother Jonathan. Angela Davis's famously large 'fro is still emblematic of the Black freedom struggle. Davis got involved in the struggle when George Jackson, John W. Cluchette, and Fleeta Drumgo got locked up. Although they weren't related to each other, they became known as the Soledad Brothers. Angela Davis was an active member of the Communist party and considered the Soledad Brothers to be prisoners of a class war. Davis's political stance had already made her a target at the University of California at Los Angeles, where she worked. In fact, she had to go to court to keep her job as a professor. So when she started giving speeches in defense of the Soledad Brothers, the California Board of Regents and Governor Ronald Reagan used the fact that she hadn't finished her PhD as justification for firing her again. That wasn't the half of it! Some of Davis's guns were used when Jonathan Jackson stormed a courthouse. He took hostages. He wound up dead, along with a judge and two prisoners. They charged Davis with kidnapping, conspiracy, and murder and placed her on the FBI's Ten Most Wanted List. That's when she went on the run. It took two months to capture her. But in the end, she was not guilty. You should look that up because that's not the end of her story.

More on the Black Intellectual and the Activist

- Rebecca Hall turned Nella Larsen's *Passing* into a screenplay for the 2021 movie by that same name.

- *Their Eyes Were Watching God* is Zora Neale Hurston's best known work, but she wrote anthropology too, like *The Sanctified Church*.

- W. E. B. Du Bois's *Souls of Black Folk* is perhaps the most important book written at the turn of the twentieth century.

- In 1949 Claudia Jones published a pamphlet called "An End to the Neglect of the Problems of the Negro Woman!" Google the title to find a downloadable PDF of it.

- If you want to think about more contemporary activism, Howard University's Law Library has a page on their website about the Black Lives Matter movement.

The Imaginary and the Visionary

ONE COULD ARGUE Black people are what they are partially because of how white people imagined them. It sounds deep and philosophical, but if you meditate on it for a while, you'll figure it out. Though everybody knows what Black people look like, it is also true that we are often not seen for who we are. We are stereotyped, racially profiled, and often made into shadows.

Imaginary and visionary folks represent the future. The fact is Black folks must be imaginary. But we also need to understand how we are imagined. We must be visionary but must also learn to see clearly.

PUBLIC SERVICE ANNOUNCEMENT
If you understand these things, folks will call you crazy.

Silent Black People

ALMOST ALL OF YOU know some Silent Black people. Given our history with slavery in the rural South, silence is not simply about what Black folks couldn't say. Some of it is about what Black folks knew to be beyond words.

You see, spiritual traditions in this country are too connected to words. In Africa and the East, silence is often one of the greatest signs of wisdom. We talk too much. Some of the silence in quiet Black people is about listening. They pay attention to other things in the world besides words: trees, wind blowing in the air at night, the coming thunder, or even just plain quiet.

Next time you see a Silent Black person, dare to ask yourself some questions about their silence. Ask yourself: What do they know that they aren't saying? What are they thinking about? Or check this one: Maybe they silent and not even thinking? Maybe silence is a sign of meditation.

Christianity

WHILE MANY AFRICAN AMERICANS point to Christianity's beginning in Africa, that seems crazy as hell. There is little doubt that, along with much of the world, African Americans were forced into the practice of Christianity. If Christians had actually been like Jesus, we might not be Christians. Jesus was not really down with taking people's money, living in all-white neighborhoods, or lynchings. And it isn't a coincidence that the Ku Klux Klan burned crosses on the lawns of African Americans who they sought to intimidate. The cross is the most sacred and resonant symbol of Christianity. The Klan—probably the longest-standing terror group in America—identifies as a Christian organization. It would have been great if some of the real serious Christians had worked out the contradictions in that kind of wayward use of their religion. Sadly, that has not been the case. Of all the things racism seems highly compatible with, Christianity may be the most popular. Then again, for even many Black folks who worship him, Jesus is white. Of course, we could say it doesn't matter whether Jesus is white or Black, but to say that in a country that has wasted so much time on the color issue might sound crazy.

Wakandans

EVEN BEFORE THE HUGELY SUCCESSFUL Marvel movie *Black Panther*, Wakandans existed. In your neighborhood or in your church, you can probably identify some Wakandans. They usually dress different, talk different, eat different food. Some of them have dreadlocks. Often Wakandans change their names. Many of our *Crazy as Hell* heroes were Wakandan before the folks came up with Wakanda. During Black History Month, the Wakandans in your community get to stand up or get imported to other communities to speak about their studies, their travels, and depending on the mood of the country, their fight against The Man.

During Black History Month, we think they're cool, but for the other eleven months of the year, we tend to think Wakandans are crazy as hell. For most of us, a Wakandan is an imaginary negro. We got regular names like white folks. We dress like regular people do. We don't have time to study Africa. After all, what good will it do when you have to live in America and deal with white folks every day? We were raised here, gotta go to work here, and have to live here.

What makes Wakandans great is the Hollywood production come to life on the big screen. It may be that all good Wakandans have a few smart white people behind them to help the fantasy go over well. We know it sounds crazy, but imagine a YouTube version of *Black Panther*. One without the special effects and real-time movie quality. We run around now crossing our arms in front of our chests behind the Disney version. But the YouTube one—without all the fancy stuff, just showing some Black Pride version—we wouldn't like that version. A movie like that might make us mad. We'd watch it and be ashamed that we just can't do stuff as good as white folks.

Hoteps

THOSE OF US WHO SPEND our lives searching through the annals of Black history for answers usually do so because our families are jacked up—because somebody Black hurt us—because somebody white hurt us. Somebody hurt us. We have been traumatized by our past, and as a result we search for answers. Trauma is difficult on the human spirit. In this regard, Hoteps are a lot like religious fanatics.

Many will say Hoteps are Black people who believe in all the negative things we won't tolerate from white people, like hatred of white people, women, and members of the LGBTQ+ community. Unlike white Christians and many other groups with such ideas built into their religions, Hoteps are arguably the most powerless. They have no media networks, just a little bit of money, and they own little property. In this way, Hoteps have become the opposite of Wakandans.

Plus, hoteps, they liable to say something crazy as hell at any moment. They will sell you a book on African American history written by a historian that Wikipedia has never heard of; they'll tell you that three of the first five presidents were Black; and then tell you DC was built on ancient Kemetic knowledge in the middle of a conversation about Black Lives Matter—like knowing about Egypt equips you with vibranium skin to protect you from an assailant's gun on a dark night.

If Wakandans act like they are from another place fit for a superhero, Hoteps act like they are headed to that place. That's a hard sell for most folks. But if you know what a Hotep is, look at white supremacists the same way. It might free up some energy for you and help you see how white supremacy is not about white superiority but rather white people's trauma.

Yo Mama

Yo mama so fat, she fell in love and broke it!
Yo mama so old, I told her to act her age and she died!
Yo mama so dumb, she put a watch in a piggy bank to save time!

"YO MAMA" JOKES MIGHTA BEEN the start of playing the dozens way back when Black people were sold on the auction block. When slaves were sold on the block, some were sold as individuals. They were skilled laborers, like carpenters or blacksmiths, or they were really strong. These people sold for more money than the average slave. Most were sold in lots of a dozen. That is where the expression *playing the dozens* comes from.

Over the years, the word for it has changed. It has been called joaning, ragging, ripping, roasting, the dozens, and other names, but it's the same thing—a battle of words. At least two people go in on each other to the delight of listeners. The point is to not lose your cool or revert to physical violence. The battle is supposed to stay verbal. This was important because enslaved people could measure intelligence and the ability to stay cool. This let them know who they could trust to outwit Massa—and who they couldn't. They talked about yo mama because under slavery, if someone was standing on the auction block, you could almost be certain they didn't have a mama. Talking about someone's mama during slavery is like telling "yo mama" jokes in an orphanage. It stings. Mainly because the only thing you really know about your mama is that she ain't there.

More on the Imaginary and the Visionary

- In the tradition of the Biblical magi, the three wise men who spotted the star in the sky marking the birth of Jesus, check out Neil deGrasse Tyson's work as an astrophysicist.

- You might like the Luke Cage comic books, which first appeared in 1972.

- *The Life & Loves of Mr. Jiveass Nigger* is an unauthorized autobiography of maybe the most adept Black man in the history of turning the imaginary into a vision for freedom.

- Check out Faith Ringgold's art.

- There are way too many novels that could fit in this category, but you might try Gloria Naylor's novel *Mama Day*, which is a really good read.

- Another really good novel is Colson Whitehead's *The Intuitionist*.

- But perhaps no one beats Octavia Butler's *Parable of the Sower* and *Parable of the Talents* for visionary novels. They are worth a read.

The White People

ANYONE DEMANDING THAT people call them Master is crazy as hell. But it makes sense when you look up the history of white folks who got on a boat to America. If the Statue of Liberty says "Give me your tired, your poor, your huddled masses yearning to breathe free," we know that at least some of the white folks who came here were not kings and queens in Europe. It wasn't the masters who got on the boat. The masterful people stayed home. Cuz they had all the best shit, and they were in charge. The folks clambering to get out of Europe were often on the bottom rung of the ladder. In fact, a good number of them weren't even clambering—they were driven onto the boats. Britain used colonial settlements as dumping grounds for people they didn't want around. In those early years, during the seventeenth and eighteenth centuries, Britain sent around 50,000 convicts to the colonies. So think about it. If you were expelled from your country, wouldn't you come up with a way to feel better about your situation? And that option was entirely possible because, after all, they sent you to a whole New World! Absolutely no one who knew your situation was around.

It would be good if more people thought about that because some of the craziest parts of Black people are the parts of white people that have soaked into our brains since we started calling folks Massa. We know that sounds crazy, but how else do you explain skin bleaching, colored contacts, spending $350 to get your hair weaved, and all the weird things in Black culture that seem like white people?

Some people say the craziest part of Black folks is the part of us that tries to act like white people. Black folks might not be as crazy as we are if white folks treated us better. We don't know if that is true. But we'll let you decide. White people kidnapped us and brought us here. Then white people talked about freedom and declared independence while they beat us, made us call them "master," and forced us to work for free. They lynched us, murdered our babies, raped us, cut off people's limbs, and told us we deserved it because we were cursed. Sounds crazy, don't it? Crazy as hell.

PUBLIC SERVICE ANNOUNCEMENT
The idea of white supremacy might completely evaporate if we become able to recognize white people's trauma. You can disarm racists right in the middle of an outburst by acknowledging whatever suffering of theirs you recognize. Consider that possibility as a viable alternative to outrage or utter helplessness the next time a Karen picks up her phone to call the po-po with some ill-founded claims.

The Man

THE MAN OFTEN REFERS TO the police, but really it operates like a pronoun referring to any white man with power and influence. It's a reduction, yet the way folks act you'd think The Man is God. That's crazy! He ain't God. He ain't even a he. The Man is an idea that one category of people is bigger and more powerful than they really are. Like The Man really do be holding folks down. Systems like redlining and gerrymandering undercut housing options and undermine voting rights. Privatization of prisons assigns a profit motive for locking people up. Stuff like that works to offer some folks a better chance at living well than others. These systems need to be dismantled. But The Man is a bogeyman running around in our waking dreams. He ain't real.

Becky

BLACK MEN WILL SAY they don't want her, but there is a reason why weave is so popular among Black women. Men want women with hair that hangs to her waist and be blowing in the wind. A lot of Black women try to have hair like Becky. But Becky don't have to buy hers. Plus she don't feel disrespected regardless of what a man says or does to her. Black women claim that they won't put up with shit. Becky be dealing with the most though. She's a trophy, a sign of accomplishment and transgression rolled into one. No matter what she built like—hourglass, pear, apple, stick—no matter what she look like, her face can look like a foot; it don't matter. You gotta watch her cause this bitch will take your man.

Karen

I KNOW LOTS OF WOMEN named Karen who are not *Karens*. Karens are not so named at birth. Instead they earn the name by acting as if whatever they desire is theirs by birthright. It seems that the number of Karens moving through the population is increasing. This is a false impression. Instead, much like the incidents of police brutality, the perception is heightened by the ubiquity of cameras. There are simply more people acting like Karens caught on camera. The thing about Karens is that they appear harmless on the surface—but ask Emmitt Till about how dangerous a Karen can be. The problem is that historically the word of one Karen carries more weight than any number of Black witnesses, which is why video is so important in spotting a Karen at work. Karens are tricky because they masquerade as victims. They exploit the implicit bias of onlookers by crying and carrying on in such a way that people watching feel compelled to act. And if no one is nearby, they summon witnesses—often by dialing 911. Karens are well aware that these phone calls will be recorded, so even if the police do not arrive, they have set the stage for acquiring allies in the most violent fashion without ever having had to strike a blow. Meanwhile, it gets crazy as hell for Black people trying to defend themselves against this type of aggression.

More on the White People

- There is a lot to read on white people in America, but you might want to check out:

- Amber Ruffin's *You'll Never Believe What Happened to Lacey.*

- Rhonda Magee's *The Inner Work of Racial Justice.*

- Kelly Brown Douglas's *Stand Your Ground: Black Bodies and the Justice of God.*

- Cheryl Harris's "Whiteness as Property."

- David Roediger is a scholar who studied whiteness for many years. Check out his work if you want to study further.

- And you might want to visit the National Museum of African American History and Culture's website where they talk about whiteness.

The Unwitting Representatives of the Anonymous Masses

BLACK HISTORY IS FULL of Black bodies because people kept killing our leaders. Martin Luther King, Jr., was killed in 1968 over his push for civil rights. Malcolm X was killed in 1965 as his perspective on race became more international, putting him in conflict with the Nation of Islam. People even say that Tupac Shakur was killed in 1996 as part of a conspiracy, which sounds crazy as hell, since he was a rapper who spent a good portion of his time rapping about his own death, always at the hands of other Black men. Rappers make songs about how the streets be killing folks all the time. But in addition to talking about hard life on the streets, like Tupac's aunt, *Crazy as Hell* shero Assata Shakur, Tupac also spoke of revolution. Maybe someone shot him because of that.

It is clear that Martin and Malcolm were assassinated because of the ideas they held. In this book, we have even gone so far as to call them crazy for thinking them. They were men whose ideas set them apart from other people. They became martyrs because of the way they used their minds. Today, really smart people often talk about "the Black body" as though Black people have no mind. It's crazy as hell to imagine a Black person without a mind, but maybe they are trying to explain how white people see the world. We can't really afford to think about it that way.

Craziness is about the mind.

But unlike Tupac or Malcolm or Martin, some of the best-known bodies in Black history did not have a public voice. While folks suggest that Martin or Malcolm or Medgar or so many others were killed because of their ideas, the history of the United

States of America suggests otherwise. White people were afraid that Black people would get better positioning.

That's why so many Black people were lynched. Lynching is a strange kind of murder that seems to swallow up the names of those who were hung from poplar trees. The age of video and social media has changed that. The journey that started in the 1960s civil rights era of television cameras capturing images of fire hoses being turned on marchers is now fully realized, as we have become a nation of cameras and surveillance. Videos of modern-day lynchings can circulate on an infinite loop via the internet, linking the victim's face and name to their killing. Then we adopt these dead as martyrs. It is as though a person who speaks about our politics and our history is harder to accept as a Black hero than a person who dies just because they are Black. It is impossible to disagree with someone when you don't know their opinion.

These are those who appear one day in the news or Facebook threads or Instagram posts or Tik Tok or YouTube videos. They rise above the noise of our everyday lives to capture our attention. The anonymous folks who we never knew when they were alive but became instant celebrities upon their sudden deaths. Of course, pictures and videos are important. Many of the folks on this list have incited rage, activism, and riots because the videos gave proof to what we already knew. In the past, word of their deaths spread through the grapevine and professional news outlets. Nowadays, we all have direct access to worldwide distribution networks via social media. We can witness murder in real time. And their dying captures our attention in ways that their living never could. Amadou Diallo, Freddie Gray, Eric Garner, Botham Jean, Atatiana Jefferson, Breonna Taylor, Ahmaud Arbery . . . There are too many to list them all here.

PUBLIC SERVICE ANNOUNCEMENT
If you become a Black history hero just because you are killed, we might be at the end of Black history.

Emmett Till

FOURTEEN-YEAR-OLD EMMETT TILL was murdered in 1955 for allegedly flirting with a white shopkeeper named Carolyn Bryant. Till was from Chicago, Illinois, and was staying with relatives in Money, Mississippi, for the summer. Till went into the Bryants' store to buy something, and when he left he said something flirtatious to Carolyn Bryant. She told folks that he had made catcalls and grabbed her. When her family heard the story, they took matters into their own hands. The murder was announced in a German newspaper headline: "The Life of a Negro Isn't Worth a Whistle."

Emmett Till's mother, Mamie Bradley, refused to close the casket during his funeral. She wanted the world to see what they had done to her son. People say that Till's murder sparked the Civil Rights Movement. That's not true. But the fact that he was so young mattered to people. Then too, after they were quickly acquitted of Till's murder, Carolyn's husband Roy Bryant and her half brother J. W. Milam had the nerve to publish a story in *Look* magazine telling how they murdered the boy. What's even crazier is that in 2017, Bryant recanted her story that Emmett Till had done anything that could have justified his murder. We'd *have* to be crazy to believe that anything he did could have justified what they did to him.

Four Little Girls

ON SUNDAY, SEPTEMBER 15, 1963, Carol Denise McNair, Cynthia Wesley, Carole Rosamond Robertson, Addie Mae Collins, and her sister Sarah were in the ladies' room before service at the 16th Street Baptist Church in Birmingham, Alabama, when a white nationalist set off an explosion. Of the five girls in the bathroom, only Sarah survived. No one was prosecuted for the murders until 1977.

The neighborhood where the church is located was called "Bombingham" because the KKK planted so much dynamite there. It's the same neighborhood that *Crazy as Hell* hero Angela Davis and former secretary of state Condoleezza Rice grew up in.

If you get a chance to visit Birmingham, Alabama, be sure to check out the Birmingham Civil Rights Institute, a museum located directly across from the 16th Street Baptist Church. There's also a park on the other side of the street with bronze sculptures depicting the city's struggle for civil rights.

Rodney King

THOUGH RODNEY KING WAS NOT KILLED, he is one of the most important people in this section. The video of King being surrounded and beaten by fourteen officers in April 1992 took police brutality into the digital age. This video seemed to be a way of prepping us for videos of Black murders more than twenty years in advance.

King's video changed the nation. As usual, the officers went unpunished, but their acquittal officially began the 1992 Los Angeles riots, which lasted for six days and resulted in numerous deaths and the destruction of hundreds of millions of dollars in property.

Some say the only reason so many people wanted *Crazy as Hell* notable O. J. Simpson to get off those murder charges is because of the Rodney King verdict.

Trayvon Martin

ON FEBRUARY 26, 2012, seventeen-year-old Trayvon Martin was walking home from the store after buying a package of Skittles and a bottle of Arizona iced tea. George Zimmerman decided Martin looked like a threat, so he followed him, killed him, and then claimed self-defense. Outrage over Martin's death sparked the Black Lives Matter movement. Zimmerman's record to that date showed he was a clear menace to society, but the crazy thing is that the criminal justice system acquitted Zimmerman for killing a kid on the basis of Florida's Stand Your Ground laws. You should google Stand Your Ground and see what states got those laws on the books and to see who gets protected by them and who gets killed.

Sandra Bland

IN JULY 2015, SANDRA BLAND was pulled over by a Texas state trooper for a minor traffic violation and wound up dead three days later in the Waller County Jail. Her death was classified as suicide by the coroner. The account of Bland's death while in custody seems a little crazy. Bland was a twenty-eight-year-old woman on her way to start a new job. Why would she commit suicide? That question, along with the repeated lies told by the arresting officer, who explained his aggression toward Bland as "fearing for his life," leaves people wondering what to make of her death. But her death got folks thinking more about mental health needs as well as strategies for de-escalation in encounters with police.

Tamir Rice

LIKE EMMITT TILL, the four little girls, and Trayvon Martin, the story of Tamir Rice breaks our hearts. He was just twelve years old. His death at such a young age lets you know how dangerous being Black can be. Next time you see a twelve-year-old, try to imagine what it means to shoot one.

Tamir was shot on November 22, 2014, at a playground in Cleveland, Ohio, by a police officer who, in a previous job, was deemed "emotionally unstable" and "unfit for duty." Still the courts found the murder of a twelve-year-old boy by a man deemed "emotionally unstable" a "justifiable homicide." Tamir was killed for playing with a toy gun. It's enough to drive you crazy.

Americans know violence and guns better than the rest of the world. We watch murder on TV, have paint gun wars, and grow up playing cops and robbers, cowboys and Indians. Almost everyone in the country has played with guns. But we live in a twilight zone where we look at a childlike Tamir and see a criminal who is so dangerous that he must be shot on sight. We know it's a twilight zone because the system protected the madman who killed rather than the child who was innocently playing.

George Floyd

GEORGE FLOYD'S LAST WORDS sounded like an eerie echo of Eric Garner's. On July 17, 2014, Eric Garner told Staten Island police eleven times: "I can't breathe." The police were arresting him for allegedly selling loose cigarettes outside a convenience store. Garner was not a little man, but when he objected to what he called harassment, the police subdued him physically. Given Garner's size and the number of officers who actually participated in his assault, ask yourself this question: What does it take for a bunch of men with guns to realize it does not require a lynch mob to subdue one Black man?

People could not help but think of Eric Garner when video emerged of George Floyd pleading with a Minneapolis cop kneeling on his neck for 9 minutes and 29 seconds. It seems kinda simple. If someone can't breathe because of some action that you are taking, and that action is avoidable, then you should stop doing that thing so that the man can breathe. Floyd's death, coming at the time of the COVID-19 pandemic, sparked worldwide outrage over the image of such a brutally unfair justice system.

More on the Unwitting Representatives of the Anonymous Masses

- Watch Spike Lee's 1997 documentary *4 Little Girls*.

- Check out the story in Time.com titled "When One Mother Defied America: The Photo That Changed the Civil Rights Movement." It's about Mamie Till publishing a photo of her son in *Jet* magazine in 1955.

- Look up the work being done by Travon Martin's mother, Sabrina Fulton.

- Amnesty International has worked for many years on matters like police violence.

- For more context on how some of these incidents occur, read about the 1967 uprising in Detroit. A good place to start is Danielle McGuire's book *The Algiers Motel Incident*.

- Famous for his activism, Mumia Abu-Jamal asks in his 2017 book published by City Lights Books *Have Black Lives Ever Mattered?*

Closing Thoughts

BLACK HISTORY SUCKS! It's painful—full of suffering and sorrow. It is tempting to look away and not think of it at all. But African Americans are undoubtedly the funkiest people on the planet! How can we ever understand why African Americans keep coming up with moves and music that connect with people all around the world if we do not pay attention to the conditions that shape the Black experience?

This book is a guide that walks us along the road between our suffering and our art. It helps to have company on this dark road. That way we know someone else understands just how crazy all this has been. Otherwise, every generation or so, we crack. Something will happen that seems one offense too many, and then we run out into the streets to break glass and burn stuff. Police show up in riot gear, and after a while the wildfire is put down and things return to smoldering.

Our entire history in this country can make you crazy.

And we keep trying to tell folks. Think about how many Black writers show the Black experience as a kind of maddening fall. Toni Morrison's first book, *The Bluest Eye*, depicts how early the psychic break begins to take hold. Pecola is a little Black girl who goes crazy because she is utterly convinced of her ugliness. And she believes that she is ugly simply because she is Black. It's not just Morrison, though. A lot of authors touch on crazy, like John Edgar Wideman's *Reuben*, LeRoi Jones's *Dutchman*, Gayl Jones's *Eva's Man*, Gloria Naylor's *Linden Hills*, Richard Wright's *Native Son*, Ralph Ellison's *Invisible Man*, Zora Neale Hurston's *Their Eyes Were Watching God* . . . and we could go on. The tradition of African American literature represents the legacy of slavery as maddening. So it's no wonder, then, that if we pull back and look at the culture more broadly, nearly all of our heroes (and some who are not so heroic) might be viewed through the lens of insanity.

We can find these crazy folks everywhere. They are in our churches, in our schools, in our neighborhoods, at our jobs, in our mirrors. Many times they attract attention because they just don't know how to act. Instead of following the rules, they make up their own, and more often than not, we are the better for it.

Glossary

13th Amendment *noun* the 13th Amendment to the United States Constitution made involuntary servitude illegal, with a couple of notable exceptions.

African retention *noun* practices and rituals that are carried with people as they become immersed in a new culture. APPLICATION: *Greek letter organizations' step dance is a retention of stomp dancing like that performed by coal miners in South Africa.*

Black Codes *noun* also known as Jim Crow laws, these were ordinances passed in the era following Reconstruction to limit the freedoms of African Americans. APPLICATION: *The grandfather clause is an example of a Black Code, which stated that only individuals whose grandfathers were registered voters could vote.*

blackface *noun* a type of makeup used in minstrel performances to blacken the complexion of the entertainer, often with exaggerated white outlines around the eyes and red lipstick to make the lips appear larger.

Bukra *noun* derived from West Africa, a term for white people used by African peoples in the Caribbean and the southeastern US.

caucasity *adj.* the unadulterated sense of entitlement of some white people to do things Black people find unimaginable, like tackling a fourteen-year-old in possession of an iPhone. APPLICATION: *After simply asking a woman to leash her dog at a bird-watching park, a Black man might think "The caucasity!" when she begins calling the police to falsely accuse him of attacking her.*

cultural appropriation *noun* the adoption of select and random aspects of a culture outside of one's own for the benefit of personal or economic interests without regard for its significance to the people from which they derived. APPLICATION: *Warner Brothers built an industry off Bugs Bunny, which is basically a cultural appropriation of an African trickster figure, and no Black people made a single nickel.*

Emancipation Proclamation *noun* a declaration penned in 1863 during the Civil War by President Abraham Lincoln that freed enslaved people in the states that had seceded from the Union. APPLICATION: *The Emancipation Proclamation is cited as the document that freed the slaves, despite the fact that technically the Proclamation didn't free anyone.*

fetish *noun* a term that emerged in the European encounter with West Africans as a label applied by white people with limited understanding of objects that according to African belief systems were endowed with power. APPLICATION: *Hoping to become pregnant, the woman acquired a fetish to wear around her neck.*

grapevine *noun* the elaborate network of gossip that works like fiber-optic phone lines for news to travel within a community. APPLICATION: *The news of his return home traveled quickly through the grapevine and reached her ears before she left work.*

Great Migration *noun* the largest movement of a cultural group in the history of the United States, from southern rural communities to urban centers in the North and West, occurring during the first half of the twentieth century with peaks during the First and Second World Wars. APPLICATION: *The Great Migration is basically the twentieth-century version of the Underground Railroad.*

Juneteenth *noun* the way the story goes is that some enslaved people living all the way in Texas had no idea that they had been freed by the Civil War until June 19, 1865, a full six months after everyone else knew the South had been defeated. Now Black folks celebrate June 19th as Independence Day. APPLICATION: *President Joe Biden declared June 19th a national holiday, so fire up the grill!*

Maafa *noun* a Kiswahili word meaning "great tragedy" that refers to the atrocity also called the Middle Passage.

maroons *noun* derived from the Spanish word "cimarrones," which means "mountaineers," the term was used first to identify the people who created covert mountain settlements after escaping Spanish-owned plantations when the British took over the island of Jamaica.

Middle Passage *noun* the long, arduous journey African captives were forced to endure across the Atlantic Ocean in the hulls of European slave ships.

minstrel *noun* a type of entertainer popularized after the Civil War, often white men performing demeaning depictions of African Americans in blackface. APPLICATION: *The college frat party turned into a minstrel show when students came dressed as their favorite athlete or entertainer.*

ooftah *noun* an expression used by the Civil Rights generation to describe Black people who pandered for white folks. APPLICATION: *Look at that ooftah over there!*

quadroon *noun* a term derived from the word *quarter* to describe a person with one Black grandparent.

root *noun* a conjured spell or hex. APPLICATION: *I'm bout to put a root on her because she is cheatin with my man.*

trickster *noun* a character or person who uses wit, cunning, and their deep understanding of human dynamics to gain advantage.

Beyond the Book

- Select one or more of the categories presented in *Crazy as Hell* for further study. Reflect on the characteristics that make the people in them appear crazy with the aim of identifying empirical evidence to support an alternative reading of what looks like crazy on an ordinary day.

- Sometimes notoriety comes from timing and opportunity. Cite specific historical laws to explain why three *Crazy as Hell* notables might be perceived differently if they lived at another time and in another place.

- Take note of the people in your community. Maybe one or two of them is crazy as hell. What are the remarkable things about them that could get them into the annuls of Black history?

- Write an essay explaining how certain individual actions press against the boundaries of social norms and result in positive collective transformation.

- Research a figure from *Crazy as Hell*, then write a monologue in their voice. The scripts generated from this writing process can be anthologized.

- Try to enumerate the dominant threads that frame the people in *Crazy as Hell*. Consider the ways that the figures are talked about in scholarly journals, major news outlets, social media, and the like. Why they are understood this way? What do these characterizations allow? What do they prevent?

- Research the history of mental asylums and the condition known as "feeblemindedness" in the United States. Then compare and contrast how that notion connects to constructions of race and gender.

- Create a thirty-minute lesson plan using *Crazy as Hell* as a resource. The lesson should include a topic, benchmarks, performance standards, learning outcomes, and a description of the learning environment and instructional activities.

- Speculate about how crazy people living in our world today might impact the way our society will operate in the future.

- Write a narrative depicting an experience you or someone you know had that was crazy as hell.

Wells Woodson

NAMED AFTER IDA B. WELLS AND CARTER G. WOODSON, ancestors who gave their lives to the struggle for survival, progress, and uplift of African American people, Wells Woodson Renaissance is a book club that cultivates knowledge through study groups; courses and curricula; and publications and programming for the purpose of enriching, informing, and activating the community. WWR began as an effort to bring together a group of knowledgable and intellectually curious friends to read books by, for, and of benefit to African Americans; build knowledge; and nurture our sense of community. Members are educators, either by profession or by the roles they choose to play in the development of communities, who:

1   Read books by, for, and of benefit to African American people

2   Contribute to discussions on issues that are pertinent to the survival, progress, and uplift of African American people

3   Attend and participate in activities and events that enrich the sense of community

4   Advance the cause of education beginning with themselves and extending to students, communities, and country

5   Practice civic engagement to develop a greater sense of social justice within American society

6   Develop and participate in strategies for survival and improvement of the lives of African American people

Freedom Reads

FREEDOM READS is a first-of-its-kind organization that empowers people through literature to confront what prison does to the spirit. With the Freedom Library and literary programs, Freedom Reads supports the efforts of people in prison to imagine new possibilities for their lives. Freedom begins with a book. For more information, go to freedomreads.org.

For information about permission to reproduce selections from this book,
write to Permissions, W. W. Norton & Company, Inc.,
500 Fifth Avenue, New York, NY 10110

For information about special discounts for bulk purchases, please contact
W. W. Norton Special Sales at specialsales@wwnorton.com or 800-233-4830

Manufacturing by Versa Press
Book design by James Goggin, Practise

Used on the front cover and for headings throughout this book, Martin is a
nonviolent typeface designed by Tré Seals, a Black designer from Washington
DC, and inspired by the Memphis Sanitation Strike of 1968. As striking workers
marched, they carried copies of a poster declaring "I AM A MAN," a statement
that recalled a question abolitionists posed more than a hundred years earlier:
"Am I not a Man and a Brother?" Martin Luther King Jr. joined the cause, speak-
ing to a crowd of six thousand in late March and returning on April 3 (the day
before his assassination) to deliver one of his most famous speeches, "I've Been
to the Mountaintop."

Freight Text and Freight Sans, used for body text in this book, started as a serif
family inspired by the warmth and pragmatism found in eighteenth-century
Dutch typefaces, designed by Joshua Darden, founder of Scanjam and Darden
Studio. Born 1979 in Los Angeles, California, Darden is the first African American
credited as a type designer. Freight has gradually expanded into a collection of
156 fonts that have the ability to be bold and daring just as easily as they can be
quiet and unassuming.

Production manager: Julia Druskin

ISBN 978-1-324-07887-6

W. W. Norton & Company, Inc.,
500 Fifth Avenue, New York, N.Y. 10110
www.wwnorton.com

W. W. Norton & Company Ltd.,
15 Carlisle Street, London W1D 3BS

1 2 3 4 5 6 7 8 9 0